TWENTIETH CENTURY VIEWS

The aim of this series is to present the best in contemporary critical opinion on major authors, providing a twentieth century perspective on their changing status in an era of profound revaluation.

Maynard Mack, *Series Editor*
Yale University

LITERATURE
OF THE OCCULT

LITERATURE
OF THE OCCULT

A COLLECTION OF CRITICAL ESSAYS

Edited by
Peter B. Messent

Prentice-Hall, Inc.   A SPECTRUM BOOK   *Englewood Cliffs, N.J.*

Library of Congress Cataloging in Publication Data
Main entry under title:

Literature of the occult.

  (Twentieth century views) (A Spectrum Book)
  Bibliography: p.
  CONTENTS: Messent, P. Introduction.—Todorov, T.
The uncanny and the marvellous.—[etc.]
    1. English fiction—History and criticism—Addresses,
essays, lectures. 2. Occultism in literature—
Addresses, essays, lectures. 3. Supernatural in
literature—Addresses, essays, lectures. 4. American
fiction—History and criticism—Addresses, essays,
lectures. I. Messent, Peter B.
PR830.O33L57   823'.009'37   80-26190
ISBN   0-13-537712-9
ISBN   0-13-537704-8 (pbk.)

Editorial/production supervision by Maria Carella
& Betty Neville.
Cover design by Vivian Berger, © 1981 by Vivian Berger
Manufacturing buyer: Barbara A. Frick

10   9   8   7   6   5   4   3   2   1

PRENTICE HALL INTERNATIONAL, INC. *(London)*
PRENTICE-HALL OF AUSTRALIA, PTY. LTD. *(Sydney)*
PRENTICE-HALL OF CANADA, LTD. *(Toronto)*
PRENTICE-HALL OF INDIA PRIVATE LIMITED *(New Delhi)*
PRENTICE-HALL OF JAPAN, INC. *(Tokyo)*
PRENTICE-HALL OF SOUTHEAST ASIA PTE. LTD. *(Singapore)*
WHITEHALL BOOKS LIMITED *(Wellington, New Zealand)*

To William and Alice

Contents

ix

H. P. Lovecraft and an American Literary Tradition

Acknowledgments

Scattered quotations from *The Fantastic* by Tzvetan Todorov are used by permission of Georges Borchardt, Inc., and Les Editions du Seuil.

Quotations from *The Idea of the Holy* by Rudolf Otto are used by permission of Oxford University Press.

The quotation from Algernon Blackwood, *Tales of Terror and the Unknown* (E.P. Dutton & Company, 1965), pp. 20-21 is reprinted by permission of the publisher, E. P. Dutton, and A. P. Watt & Son.

The excerpt from *The Roots of Horror in the Fiction of H. P. Lovecraft* by Barton Levi St. Armand on pp. 15-16 is used by kind permission of Dragon Press, 153 Deerfield Lane, Pleasantville, N.Y. 10570.

The excerpt from Douglas Boyd, *Rolling Thunder*—copyright © 1974 by Robert Briggs Associates—is used by permission of Random House, Inc.

Excerpts from John Dickson Carr, *The Burning Court*—copyright 1937 by John Dickson Carr—are reprinted by permission of Harper & Row, Publishers, Inc., and David Higham Associates Limited.

The quotation from H. P. Lovecraft, "Arthur Jermyn," which appears in *Dagon and Other Macabre Tales,* is used by kind permission of Arkham House Publishers, Inc., Sauk City, Wisconsin.

Quotations from *Black Elk Speaks* by John G. Neihardt are used by permission of the John G. Neihardt Trust. It is published by Pocket Books Division of Simon & Schuster; a deluxe edition is available from the University of Nebraska Press.

The excerpt on page 164 from H. P. Lovecraft, *Supernatural Horror in Literature* (New York: Dover Publications, Inc., 1973) is used by kind permission of the publisher.

LITERATURE
OF THE OCCULT

Introduction

by Peter Messent

I

In this introduction* I offer a tentative definition of what goes to make up occult literature and examine some of the common concerns of this genre.[1] I have chosen to make the Gothic novel, or at least that branch of the Gothic which introduces the supernatural as an unexplained—and rationally unexplainable—phenomenon, my starting point here. Montague Summers, in his introduction to *The Supernatural Omnibus,* charts earlier appearances of the paranormal in literature, and Frances A. Yates, in *The Occult Philosophy in the Elizabethan Age,* examines literary interest in the occult in that period. However, with the consistent use and importance of the supernatural in Gothic fiction and the type of thematic concerns introduced therein, an occult literary tradition is established which, as my introduction and the essays I include here on the Gothic suggest, has continued unbroken to the present day. I have delimited my field of study in the collection to fiction rather than include drama or poetry for reasons both of length and of overall coherence, and recognize accordingly its limitations as an initial study. The poetry of the occult in particular merits both separate status and treatment.[2]

*I would like to express my warmest thanks to Dr. Murray for the helpful advice and the friendship he gave me while I was writing this introduction. The ideas which he offered provide the basis for several of the critical points I make here, and I would like to make full acknowledgment of that fact.

[1]The occult, of course, is more than just a subject for literary treatment. A useful and comprehensive bibliographical guide to modern occultism generally is to be found in *The Journal of Popular Culture,* Vol. 5, No. 3 (Winter, 1971), pp. 726/98-754/126. Written by Robert Galbreath, it is entitled "A History of Modern Occultism: A Bibliographical Survey."

[2]*The New York Literary Forum,* Vol. 4 (1980), provides a very useful comple-

Farrell comments perceptively in Peter Beagle's humorous work *Lila the Werewolf,* "You could have either werewolves or Pyrex nine-cup percolators in the world, but not both, surely." This tension between what Sir Walter Scott called in his introduction to Walpole's *The Castle of Otranto* the "appeal to that secret and reserved feeling of love for the marvellous and supernatural, which occupies a hidden corner in almost every one's bosom" and "the dissipating sights and sounds of everyday life," lies at the very foundation of occult literature.

Coleridge used his phrase "willing suspension of disbelief" with direct application to the sense of the supernatural, and in doing so posited two entirely separate worlds, that of Pyrex percolators and that of werewolves, if you like. I would suggest that, in its purest form, the literature of the occult operates in that area where these two worlds clash head on—that sense of radical disjunction, that *thrill,* the sensation of numbing dislocation which arises at that point of intersection between two separate worlds, the material and the supernatural. It is this sense of *fracture* which provides the real power of this type of literature. This sensation is equivalent in some regards to that which Richard Wilbur finds in different form in Edgar Allan Poe's "Dream-Land" with its

> Bottomless vales and boundless floods,
> And chasms, and caves, and Titan woods, ...
> Mountains toppling evermore
> Into seas without a shore; ....

Wilbur analyzes what occurs when the reader is confronted with those initial words: "The factual sense of the word 'vale' is instantly blasted by the adjective 'bottomless.'" Poe, Wilbur claims, short-circuits the intellect by his use of language, "inviting a mystic illumination," transporting the reader to "a realm of unimaginable unities in which 'bottomless' and 'vale' are compatible."

This same "blasting" of the reader is what occurs in occult fiction, but here no "realm of unimaginable unities" results. The dis-

---

mentary study to this collection. This issue, entitled *The Occult in Language and Literature,* concentrates mainly on those areas left unexamined in this series of essays—occult drama and poetry—focusing primarily on European literature. Here, I restrict my subject matter, by and large, to the English and American literary tradition.

tinction between natural and supernatural remains absolutely apparent—indeed, becomes the very *point* of the genre. This separation lies at the heart of perhaps the most widespread form of occult fiction, the ghost story. In such stories we move from that solid matter-of-factness which goes to make up the convention we call realism—in Henry James's words, "the lawn and the bright flowers and the crunch of my wheels on the gravel and the clustered tree tops over which the rooks circled and cawed"—to jarring superimpositions of the world of the other—"a view of the back of the tapestry," as the governess in James's *Turn of the Screw* calls it. That phrase will serve to sum up the method of occult literature: in terms of normal and paranormal, it makes both sides of the tapestry equally visible; and when these sides *touch* the dislocating effect occurs.

To illustrate with two examples: In Jasper John's "The Seeker of Souls" the opening paragraph presents us with two worlds, the visible and the normal and the invisible and occult, both equally "there" but separate:

> It was in a deathly silence that we awaited the coming of the hour that would release the evil thing. I heard someone cough, and it echoed through the house. The clock ticked away the minutes with a grim satisfaction, and my neighbour breathed in a noisy fashion. But for once I was grateful for both sounds; they were something ordinary and commonplace, belonging to everyday life.

Despite an element of cliché which intrudes here and elsewhere ("Philip had heard whisperings of ghosts,...but what Englishman could believe those things?"), the discontinuity between the two worlds becomes evident within the sentence structure itself. The "evil thing" and the "ordinary and commonplace" command our attention from the start. When the two worlds meet, when the "evil thing" in this case actually appears in the mundane setting, the literature of the occult exercises its characteristic effect.

In Edith Nesbit's "Man Size in Marble," these properties of the traditional ghost story are again present. There is the ritual insistence on "the truth" of the episode to be recounted, even though the narrator expects disbelief from a skeptical audience: "Although every word of this story is as true as despair, I do not expect people to believe it. Nowadays [the story was published in 1893] a 'rational explanation' is required before belief is possible."

Next, the tale itself gives us a young honeymoon couple living in
an ivy-covered cottage in a small village—the homely and mundane stratum, as in "The Seeker of Souls." In the local church,
however, lie marble figures of knights in full armor, knights who,
as

> the peasants told of them,...had been guilty of deeds so foul that
> the house they had lived in—the big house, by the way, that had
> stood on the site of our cottage—had been stricken by lightning and
> the vengeance of Heaven. But for all that, the gold of their heirs
> had bought them a place in the church.

Not, be it noted, a place that could *contain* them. On All Saints'
Eve, as the peasants liked to put it, "them two bodies sits up on
their slabs, and gets off of them, and then walks down the aisle,
in their marble" to go back to their old home.[3] If anyone should
meet them in the process, it is suggested, something disastrous
would occur—its nature remaining typically ill defined.

All Saints' Eve, the witching hour, comes. The narrator fails to
take the precautions laid down by folk tradition to ward off the
approach of evil. He visits the local church by moonlight to find
with a sickening shock that the "bodies drawed out man-size"
are gone, and their marble slabs lie "bare." Rushing home, filled
with intimations of disaster, he collides with the local doctor. He,
with his "six feet of common sense," insists that the narrator has
imagined the whole thing, and, sure enough, on returning to the
church, they find the "two shapes" lying on their slabs—one of
them, however, lacking a hand. The protagonist's mind is eased
by the sight of the figures, but when he returns home he finds
doors open, candles blazing, his wife dead, a "look of frantic fear
and horror on her face"—her hands tightly clenched. The
climactic last lines of the story give the final turn of the occult
screw:

> When I was quite sure that she was dead, and that nothing mat-
> tered at all any more, I let [the doctor] open her hand to see what
> she held. It was a grey marble finger.

[3]This intrusion of the colloquial is a common touch found in much occult
fiction. The superstitious, unsophisticated, ill-educated but "canny" local in-
habitant who manages at least to survive the uncanny occurrence itself is set
against the supposedly better-educated, but often fated "outsider" entering a
community, whose way of life he or she does not share.

It is here, at the very last, that the two worlds—natural and supernatural—*collide*. Neither world would appear to admit the other, but there we are, left finally with a cold and tangible object, the presence of which cannot be rationally explained. Through persuading the reader, nonetheless, of this presence (in this case and in that of the majority of ghost stories) the literature of the occult achieves its point.

II

If, then, occult literature stems initially from a point of intersection between "realistic" and rationally "unexplainable."[4] it obviously has a relation to the fantastic, a more inclusive type of literature defined by Tzvetan Todorov in *The Fantastic: A Structural Approach to a Literary Genre*. Difficulties with generic definitions are of course legion, and the essays selected for this collection will be found to use a wide variety of overlapping terms: the supernatural, the uncanny, the marvelous, the mysterious, the fantastic, the macabre, the unseen, even the quasi-mystical. Todorov's impressive analysis of the fantastic and of the concept of literary genres ("precisely those relay-points by which the work assumes a relation with the universe of literature") provides us with an excellent starting point for fixing the literature of the occult within a larger context.

Todorov's initial definition of the fantastic is as follows:

> In a world which is indeed our world, the one we know, a world without devils, sylphides or vampires, there occurs an event which cannot be explained by the laws of this same familiar world.

Two choices remain open then. Either the protagonist who experiences this event is "a victim of an illusion of the senses" or the event really took place: "it is an integral part of reality—but... this reality is controlled by laws unknown to us."

[4]In terms of the individual personality, this tension is to be found, I suggest, in one particular type of occult literature, the tale of the doppelgänger. In Poe's "William Wilson," Stevenson's *Dr. Jekyll and Mr. Hyde,* and Wilde's *Picture of Dorian Grey,* the forces of sanity, civilization, and repression are set directly against those of instinct, the unconscious, the anarchic. It is at the point where these two force fields meet that the supernatural is introduced, as portrait —for example—meets persona.

The fantastic occupies the duration of...[our] uncertainty. Once we choose one answer or the other, we leave the fantastic for a neighboring genre, the uncanny or the marvelous.

In the section of Todorov's book included here, these two neighboring genres are distinguished. In the uncanny,[5]

events are related which may be readily accounted for by the laws of reason, but which are, in one way or another, incredible, extraordinary, shocking, disturbing, or unexpected.

In the marvelous, the story ends

with an acceptance of the supernatural, ...supernatural elements provoke no particular reaction in either the characters or in the implicit reader. It is not an attitude toward the events described which characterizes the marvelous, but the nature of these events.

Todorov then distinguishes two subgenres lying *between* the three forms already mentioned: the "fantastic-uncanny" and the "fantastic-marvelous."

The literature of the occult may be defined, in direct relation to this latter "fantastic-marvelous," as a genre which deals with events occurring "in a world which is indeed our world": events which *shock*, which cannot be explained according to "the natural laws of this same familiar world," yet do take place. Such a genre, like Todorov's "fantastic," may then shade off in two quite different directions.

For first, of course, the occult phenomenon may be presented with a certain ambiguity. In such tales as James's *Turn of the Screw*, Le Fanu's "Green Tea," Poe's "Fall of the House of Usher," and Lovecraft's "Rats in the Wall," the reader is left hanging between a supernatural and a psychological interpretation of the events presented. Is the governess in James's story, for example, a reliable witness? Are the ghosts of Peter Quint and Miss Jessel really *there* or merely products of her overwrought imagination? No conclusive answer can be given to these questions. In Todorov's terms, the fantastic-marvelous is replaced here by the

[5]Freud has written an important essay on "'The Uncanny'" inwhich he examines this concept as it appears in E. T. A. Hoffman's story "The Sand Man." t his essay is to be found in *The Standard Edition of the Complete Psychological Works of Sigmund Freud*, Volume 17: *An Infantile Neurosis and Other Works* (London; Hogarth Press and Institute of Psycho-Analysis, 1955), pp. 217-56.

"fantastic" itself, which depends for its effect on exactly this kind of ambiguity. This is one way in which the "pure" occult may be modified.

Another category of fictions shades off in the direction of what we know as romance. But here a distinction becomes necessary. One type of romance, a type that falls *outside* the category of the occult, is described by Hawthorne in his "Custom House" introduction to *The Scarlet Letter*. Writing of "moonlight" as the "medium the most suitable for a romance writer," he goes on to observe:

> There is the little domestic scenery of the well-known apartment, the chairs, with each its separate individuality; the centre-table, sustaining a work-basket, a volume or two....all these details, so completely seen, are so spiritualized by the unusual light, that they seem to lose their actual substance. ... Nothing is too small or too trifling to undergo this change. ... A child's shoe; the doll, seated in her little wicker carriage,...whatever, in a word, has been used or played with during the day is now invested with a quality of strangeness and remoteness, though still almost as vividly present as by daylight. Thus, therefore, the floor of our familiar room has become *a neutral territory somewhere between the real world and fairyland, where the Actual and the Imaginary may meet, and each imbue itself with the nature of the other. Ghosts might enter here without affrighting us.* [My emphasis]

What Hawthorne suggests is that romance, in this sense, can bridge the gap between natural and supernatural, actual and imaginary. The material world evaporates as we enter that "neutral territory" where the distinction between realistic and supernatural becomes ambiguous. This type of romance belongs to fantasy, that area where the solid substance of everyday life disappears, where actual probabilities give way to a world in which real and fantastic shimmer together and imagination becomes more central than fact.

Occult literature on the contrary insists on the *fracture* between real and supernatural. It therefore includes only that form of romance—"a new species of romance," Walpole called it— which insists on this consciousness of dislocation. When "imagination and improbability" intrude violently upon "a strict adherence to common life" (to modify Walpole's terms somewhat), we reach the species of romance which is found within, if to one side of, my definition of occult literature. So, for example, in *Dracula,* as in *The Castle of Otranto,* exotic settings, atmospheric effects, and a style of character depiction which we associate with the romantic do not finally destroy the occult effects produced within the texts. Indeed, this type of romance pays a great deal of attention to furnishings, the actual materials which go to make up the presented world—the description, right down to *"Whitaker's Almanac,"* of the English books in the count's library in *Dracula,* for example. Once we are placed in such a world of predictable possibility as these particulars suggest, we are prepared for the dislocatory thrill that results when the unpredictable—be it gigantic helmet or living dead—intrudes. Though the environmental trappings and atmospheric effects used in this kind of romantic fiction diminish the gap between natural and supernatural, and therefore the degree of occult disjunction, that disjunction is still clearly present. Hence this type of romance belongs within the genre.

III

The stress placed in occult fiction on the "sights and sounds of everyday life" explains my inclusion in this collection of Howard Kerr's essay "'Ghosts and Ghost-Seeing': Spiritualism in American Occult Fiction" and John R. Reed's "The Occult in Later Victorian Literature." For the subject matter of spiritualism fits directly into my conception of occult literature in a way denied to the Christian literary tradition, indeed to the literature of religion generally. Spiritualism is concerned, not with formal codes of belief, but with phenomenal apparitions.[6]

The stage properties of the spiritualist meeting—revolving tables, accordions playing, bodies levitating, apparitions, and the like—all insist upon exactly that meeting of two separate worlds,

[6]Spiritualists place material and spiritual on the same plane. Thus their assertion that departed spirits continually intrude upon this world emphasizes just that point of intersection between natural and supernatural at which the occult becomes manifest. The stress of religious literature, on the other hand, is on the spiritual and *transcendent* rather than on the co-presence of supernatural and natural.

the material and the other, which constitutes the occult. The radical disharmony which occurs in these convergences of visible and invisible was effectively—if ironically—formulated by John Delaware Lewis in *Once a Week* (August 18, 1860) where he asked:

> Are the secrets of the invisible world, concealed for so many thousands of years from mortal ken, now for the first time to be made plain to us through the agency of our household furniture? Are mahogany tables the apostles of the new faith, and brass bells and accordions its missionaries? Will an outlay of ten shillings and sixpence, and the engagement of a celebrated medium, procure for us an interview with the soul of a departed father, mother, husband, wife, in the midst of a London drawing-room, with the Hansom cabs rattling outside, and the servants standing in waiting with the tray of sandwiches and sherry?

Secrets of the invisible world circulating among trays of sandwiches and sherry! This is the crossroads where occult literature thrives. On the same grounds, the whole literature of werewolves, vampirism, and other assorted monsters fits the genre, provided means are given by which the abnormal may be measured against the normal. This suggests the reason why the most successful monsters in the history of the horror movie tend to be those most recognizably human, the human image then drastically distorted physically (Karloff's Frankenstein monster) or physiologically (Lugosi's Count Dracula).

In Stoker's *Dracula,* tension between the expected and the unexpected is developed as "Kodak views" of the estate at Purfleet are discussed by the brisk though rather uncomfortable young Englishman Jonathan Harker in the exotically furnished, vast ruined castle of Count Dracula, Transylvanian aristocrat. The tension grows of course as Dracula is shown in action in a nineteenth-century Victorian setting, and the occult powers of the undead are set directly against the powers of Van Helsing, philosopher and metaphysician—"one of the most advanced scientists of his day"—protector of the sexual, moral, and social norms of the society. As Mark Hennelly points out in "*Dracula:* The Gnostic Quest and Victorian Wasteland," Dracula is in many ways an alter ego of Van Helsing; likewise the occult world of

Count Dracula is in many ways a direct representation of the nightside of the Victorian consciousness. The placing of the supernatural against the natural reverberates throughout the entire fiction, an opposition extending beyond the story to take in alternative visions of both society and morality. "Occultism is the philosophy of hidden matters," the *Encyclopedia Americana's* definition begins. Vampirism in *Dracula* is thus an entry point into an entire alternative universe. The journey to Dracula's castle begins, as Leonard Wolf suggests in his *Dream of Dracula: In Search of the Living Dead,* with

> the voyage of a candid, clear-eyed, honest Englishman [who is] moving deeper and deeper into a psychological landscape in which darkness, deceit and ancient superstition are as natural as breathing.

In literature of the occult the supernatural is more often associated with the powers of darkness than with those of light. The reality at the very core of this kind of fiction is the power of the diabolic to show itself and effectively disrupt the normal patterns of life, set against the power of the human mind to deny and combat such disruption. Images of disaster are never far from the surface. Matthew Lewis's novel *The Monk,* for example, climaxes with a powerful demonic agency bringing ruin:

> Darting his talons into the monk's shaven crown, he sprang with him from the rock. The caves and mountains rang with Ambrosio's shrieks. The daemon continued to soar aloft, till reaching a dreadful height, he released the sufferer. Headlong fell the monk through the airy waste: the sharp point of a rock received him; and he rolled from precipice to precipice, till, bruised and mangled, he rested on the river's banks.

Ambiguities of power lie very much at the heart of this fiction. Power struggles between God and the Devil, or, to offer a secular and peculiarly contemporary parallel, between forces of sanity, rationality, and stability and what might be called, in Pynchon's terms, "the brute Other," are obsessively traced. The Faustian pact (with its concomitant, the search for secret knowledge) is one of the staples of the genre. G. R. Thompson, in "A Dark

Romanticism: In Quest of a Gothic Monomyth," defines the Gothic as "demonic-quest romance," and this suggestion of a demonic quest pervades the entire field of occult literature. The role of magician, transformed, as the processes of the natural universe became more comprehensible, into that of scientist, has always been associated with power—a power which attempts to penetrate to the heart of the mystery of the universe, a power too which seeks mastery over the minds and hearts of others.

This concern evidences itself clearly in Mary Shelley's *Frankenstein*. This story, like Stevenson's *Dr. Jekyll and Mr. Hyde* and Arthur Machen's "Novel of the White Powder," lies on the boundary line and combines the characteristics of two genres, science fiction and the occult. Similarly, Victor Frankenstein bridges in his education two worlds, the occult ("secret stores of knowledge" revealed in the works of Paracelsus and of Cornelius Agrippa, author of *De Occulta Philosophia libri tres*) and the "enlightened and scientific." In fact, Frankenstein brings the methods of science to the matter of the occult. Soon convinced of the uselessness of the ancient system whose powers he now sees to be "chimerical," he is still impressed by its objectives: to seek "immortality and power; such views, although futile, were grand." He therefore undertakes to see what can be done with the new science of modern chemistry:

> The ancient teachers of this science...promised impossibilities and performed nothing. The modern masters promise very little; they know that metals cannot be transmuted, and that the elixir of life is a chimera. But these philosophers, whose hands seem only made to dabble in dirt, and their eyes to pour [sic] over the microscope or crucible, have indeed performed miracles. They penetrate into the recesses of nature, and shew how she works in her hiding places. They ascend into the heavens; they have discovered how the blood circulates, and the nature of the air we breathe. They have acquired new and almost unlimited powers; they can command the thunders of heaven, mimic the earthquake, and even mock the invisible world with its own shadows.

Frankenstein uses the techniques of "modern chemistry," though these techniques remain remarkably unspecified, to accomplish the grand designs of the occultists:

> I succeeded in discovering the cause of generation and life; nay,
> more, I became myself capable of bestowing animation upon life-
> less matter.

Science fiction is described by Todorov as "the supernatural...
explained in a rational manner but according to laws which contemporary science does not acknowledge." If we accept this
definition, we can see that Frankenstein fits it only partially. The
supernatural—the "abhorred monster"—is brought into existence scientifically, by purely human hands, but the lack of any
real scientific detail, the use of the language not of science but of
the occult ("I...disturbed with profane fingers, the tremendous
secrets of the human frame"), and, most of all, the infusion of
the monster with "spirit"— something absolutely unexplainable
by scientific law—leads the reader back to those occult sciences
to which previous reference has been made. Frankenstein's
grand scheme—to create human life itself—and the "power"
which is a direct consequence of this are presented throughout
the remainder of the book not in scientific but in diabolic terms.
An alternative to divine creation is offered as Frankenstein infuses "a spark of being" into mere "lifeless matter." His monster
then stalks the pages of the novel disrupting normal patterns of
individual and family life and placed in a relationship with his
master directly patterned, as Harold Bloom suggests, on that
between Satan and God in *Paradise Lost.* The presentation of the
relationship between monster and master—

> I am thy creature and I will be even mild and docile to my natural
> lord and king, if thou wilt also perform thy part, the which thou
> owest me. ... Remember that I am thy creature: I ought to be thy
> Adam; but I am rather the fallen angel, whom thou drivest from
> joy for no misdeed.

—and the portrayal of Victor Frankenstein's dark powers consistently imply a diabolic context. This particular "fallen angel,"
and his creator who ("like the archangel who aspired to omni-
potence") ends up "chained in an eternal hell," belong first and
foremost to occult rather than science-fiction traditions. The
latter, to use Kingsley Amis's definition,

> treat of a situation that could not arise in the world we know, but
> which is hypothesised on the basis of some innovation in science

or technology, or pseudo-science or pseudo-technology, whether human or extra-terrestrial in origin.

Obviously there is a crucial distinction to be made between "some innovation in science" and the living, breathing, anguished monster seen in Mary Shelley's novel. Yet the line between the occult and the scientific remains here a narrow one.

In both *Frankenstein* and *Dracula* the concept of a power struggle between universal forces of darkness and light is accented by the figure of the alien, a figure whose features have distinguished occult literature from *Melmoth the Wanderer* to Anne Rice's *Interview with the Vampire.* Devendra P. Varma in his article "Quest of the Numinous: the Gothic Flame" describes as one type of Gothic villain

> the terrible "superman" whose ways lie in darkness and whose strength originates far beyond mortal thoughts. He is a new mintage of the Satan portrayed by Milton in *Paradise Lost*—the immortal outcast, a masterful, vaunting villain, his spirit unbroken even in defeat. He is the Rosicrucian, the Alchemist staking his very life on some dark hope, and behind him is all the mystery of Cabbala, Freemasonry, Medieval Satanism.

One branch of occult literature derives from the Gothic in its continuing use of this "immortal outcast," this "masterful, vaunting villain." Where the hidden forces of the universe are gathered up into a human or quasi-human figure such as Frankenstein or Dracula, the status of the figure as "outsider" is insisted on throughout the text. Thus Frankenstein's experiment with the monster shatters his own connections with the "magnetic chain of humanity"[7]: he is left metaphorically tied to his grotesque creation, pursuer and pursued symbiotically linked in that Arctic wasteland in which their story ends. At the same time, one must not overlook the fact that here and in much other occult fiction a curiously ambivalent stance, containing elements of both sympathy and repulsion, is taken toward the dark protagonist as he embarks on what G. R. Thompson calls, in relation to Gothic fiction as a whole, his "metaphysical quest."

[7]Hawthorne's phrase, taken from "Ethan Brand," has, of course, its own particular occult connotations in mesmerism.

Dracula, too, is the very image of the "terrible 'superman'" of which Varma speaks; as Van Helsing informs his colleagues:

> This vampire which is amongst us in of himself so strong in person as twenty men; he is of cunning more than mortal, for his cunning be the growth of ages; he have still the aids of necromancy,... he is devil in callous, and the heart of him is not; he can, within limitations, appear at will when, and where, and in any of the forms that are to him; he can, within his range, direct the elements,... if we fail in this our fight he must surely win; and then where end we?...to fail here, is not mere life or death. It is that we henceforward become foul things of the night like him—without heart or conscience, preying on the bodies and the souls of those we love best. To us forever are the gates of heaven shut....We go on for all time abhorred by all; a blot on the face of God's sunshine; an arrow in the side of Him who died for man.

The terminology used in this novel consistently opposes the diabolic to the Christian. Dracula, alien to all conventional familial, social, and sexual patterns, has a terrible strength which threatens a supernatural disruption of what we call normality.

This disruption assumes another form in the ghost story and in those tales of horror which involve the entry into the world of normality of some supernatural presence. Jack Sullivan's thesis about the ghost story in his *Elegant Nightmares: The English Ghost Story from Le Fanu to Blackwood*, a selection from which is reprinted in this collection, can usefully be extended to take in a large number of tales of supernatural horror. Sullivan suggests that in those mysterious forces which haunt and sometimes terrorize the protagonists of such tales, we have a manifestation of a "principle of disorder" that gradually dismembers "the narrator's comfortably structured world":

> The ghost story...begins by assuming that life is rational and morally ordered, then begins to worry about that assumption when something inexplicably threatening creeps in.

We move here from the idea of a universe in which the angelic and the diabolic are at battle to a concept perhaps more suited to the modern age, that human forms of order are in fact continually threatened by the chaotic and anarchic forces of a hostile and random universe—another version perhaps of Henry Adams's view of Chaos as "the law of nature," Order as "the dream of man."

Sullivan's piece examines this thesis in depth in relation to Joseph Le Fanu's "Green Tea."

Throughout the history of occult writing, efforts have occasionally been made to define the emotions to which it appeals and which it feeds. H. P. Lovecraft's extended essay "Supernatural Horror in Literature," a part of which is included here, concentrates on this particular aspect of the occult tale, making the decisive test

> whether there be excited in the reader a profound sense of dread, ...a subtle attitude of awed listening, as if for the beating of black wings or the scratching of outside shapes and entities on the known universe's utmost rim.

Mrs. Radcliffe anticipates this conclusion, using for her test the writer's ability to move beyond terror to horror:

> They must be men of very cold imaginations with whom certainty is more terrible than surmise. Terror and horror are so far opposite, that the first expands the soul, and wakens the faculties to a high degree of life; the other contracts, freezes, and nearly annihilates them. I apprehend that neither Shakespeare nor Milton by their fictions, nor Mr. Burke by his reasoning, anywhere looked to positive horror as a source of the sublime, though they all agree that terror is a very high one; and where lies the great difference between horror and terror, but in uncertainty and obscurity, that accompany the first respecting the dreader evil?[8]

More recently, Barton Levi St. Armand in *The Roots of Horror in the Fiction of H. P. Lovecraft* has usefully expanded and developed Mrs. Radcliffe's definitions, claiming that both terror and horror are equally "annihilating" emotions:

> Terror expands the soul outward; it leads us to or engulfs us in the sublime, the immense, the cosmic. We are, as it were, lost in the ocean of fear or plunged directly into it, drowning of our dread. What we lose is the sense of self. That feeling of "awe," which traditionally accompanies intimations of the sublime, links terror with experiences that are basically religious in nature, like those annihilating confrontations with the numinous that Otto explores in *The Idea of the Holy*, ...horror is equally annihilating, but from a dramatically different direction. Horror overtakes the soul from

---

[8]"On the Supernatural in Poetry", *New Monthly Magazine*, Volume 7, (1826), pp. 149-50.

the inside; consciousness shrinks or withers from within, and the self is not flung into the exterior ocean of awe but sinks in its own bloodstream, choked by the alien salts of its inescapable prevertebrate heritage.

The intrusion, then, of the mysterious, the other, the supernatural within the context of everyday life; the clash between rational and irrational, dark forces and light; the knowledge through direct revelation of a universe directed by forces beyond our comprehension; a state of the emotions that may itself be a conflict between elements positive and negative: these factors characterize a form of literature which, as the following essays suggest, has in a curiously tenacious manner continued to hear the "scratching of outside shapes...on the known universe's utmost rim."

The Uncanny and the Marvelous

by Tzvetan Todorov

The fantastic...lasts only as long as a certain hesitation: a hesitation common to reader and character, who must decide whether or not what they perceive derives from "reality" as it exists in the common opinion. At the story's end, the reader makes a decision even if the character does not; he opts for one solution or the other, and thereby emerges from the fantastic. If he decides that the laws of reality remain intact and permit an explanation of the phenomena described, we say that the work belongs to another genre: the uncanny. If, on the contrary, he decides that new laws of nature must be entertained to account for the phenomena, we enter the genre of the marvelous.

The fantastic therefore leads a life full of dangers, and may evaporate at any moment. It seems to be located on the frontier of two genres, the marvelous and the uncanny, rather then to be an autonomous genre. One of the great periods of supernatural literature, that of the Gothic novel, seems to confirm this observation. Indeed, we generally distinguish, within the literary Gothic, two tendencies: that of the supernatural explained (the "uncanny"), as it appears in the novels of Clara Reeves and Ann Radcliffe; and that of the supernatural accepted (the "marvelous"), which is characteristic of the works of Horace Walpole, M. G. Lewis, and Maturin. Here we find not the fantastic in the strict sense, only genres adjacent to it. More precisely, the effect of the fantastic is

"The Uncanny and the Marvelous." From *The Fantastic: A Structural Approach to a Literary Genre* by Tzvetan Todorov (Cleveland, London: The Press of Case Western Reserve University, 1973), pp. 41-57. Translated from the French by Richard Howard. Copyright © 1973 by the Press of Case Western Reserve University. The chapter reprinted here has been slightly edited. Reprinted by permission of Georges Borchardt, Inc., and Les Editions du Seuil.

certainly produced, but during only a portion of our reading: in Ann Radcliffe, up to the moment when we are sure that everything which has happened is susceptible of a rational explanation; in M. G. Lewis, up to the moment when we are sure that the supernatural events will receive *no* explanation. Once we have finished reading, we understand—in both cases— that what we call the fantastic has not existed.

We may ask how valid a definition of genre may be if it permits a work to "change genre" by a simple sentence like: "At this moment, he awakened and saw the walls of his room. ..." But there is no reason not to think of the fantastic as an evanescent genre. Such a category, moreover, has nothing exceptional about it. The classic definition of the *present,* for example, describes it as a pure limit between the past and the future. The comparison is not gratuitous: the marvelous corresponds to an unknown phenomenon, never seen as yet, still to come—hence to a future; in the uncanny, on the other hand, we refer the inexplicable to known facts, to a previous experience, and thereby to the past. As for the fantastic itself, the hesitation which characterizes it cannot be situated, by and large, except in the present.

Here we also are faced with the problem of the work's unity. We take this unity as self-evident, and we assert that a sacrilege has been committed when cuts are made. But matters are probably more complicated; let us not forget that in school, where our first, and decisive, experience of literature occurred, we read only "selected passages" or "extracts" from most works. A certain fetishism of the book survives in our own day and age: the literary work is transformed both into a precious and motionless object and into a symbol of plentitude, and the act of cutting it becomes an equivalent of castration. How much freer was the attitude of a Khlebnikov, who composed his poems out of fragments of preceding poems and who urged his editors and even his printers to revise his text! Only an identification of the book with its author explains our horror of cuts.

If we do decide to proceed by examining certain parts of the work in isolation, we discover that by temporarily omitting the end of the narrative we are able to include a much larger number of texts within the genre of the fantastic. The modern (French or English) editions of *The Saragossa Manuscript* precisely confirm this: without its end, which resolves the hesitation, the book clearly belongs to the fantastic. Charles Nodier, one of the pioneers of the fantastic in France, thoroughly understood this, and deals with it in one of his tales, "Inès de las Sierras." This text consists of two apparently equal parts, and the end of the first part leaves us in utter perplexity: we are at a loss to explain the strange phenomena which occur; on the other hand, we are not as ready to admit the supernatural as we are to embrace the natural. The narrator hesitates between two procedures: to break off his narrative (and remain in the fantastic) or to continue (and abandon it). His own preference, he declares to his hearers, is to stop, with the following justification: "Any other outcome would be destructive to my story, for it would change its nature."

Yet it would be wrong to claim that the fantastic can exist only in a part of the work, for here are certain texts which sustain their ambiguity to the very end, i.e., even beyond the narrative itself. The book closed, the ambiguity persists. A remarkable example is supplied by Henry James' tale "The Turn of the Screw," which does not permit us to determine finally whether ghosts haunt the old estate, or whether we are confronted by the hallucinations of a hysterical governess victimized by the disturbing atmosphere which surrounds her. In French literature, Mérimée's tale "La Vénus d'Ille" affords a perfect example of this ambiguity. A statue seems to come alive and to kill the bridegroom; but we remain at the point of "seems," and never reach certainty.

Whatever the case, we cannot exclude from a scrutiny of the fantastic either the marvelous or the uncanny, genres which it overlaps. But we must not, on the other hand, forget Louis Vax's remark that "an ideal art of the fantastic must keep to indecision."

Let us take a closer look, then, at these two neighbors. We find that in each case, a transitory sub-genre appears: between the fantastic and the uncanny on the one hand, between the fantastic and the marvelous on the other. These sub-genres include works that sustain the hesitation characteristic of the true fantastic for a long period, but that ultimately end in the marvelous or in the uncanny. We may represent these sub-divisions with the help of the following diagram:

uncanny	*fantastic-uncanny*	*fantastic-marvelous*	*marvelous*

The fantastic in its pure state is represented here by the median line separating the fantastic-uncanny from the fantastic-marvelous. This line corresponds perfectly to the nature of the fantastic, a frontier between two adjacent realms.

Let us begin with the fantastic-uncanny. In this sub-genre events that seem supernatural throughout a story receive a rational explanation at its end. If these events have long led the character and the reader alike to believe in an intervention of the supernatural, it is because they have an unaccustomed character. Criticism has described, and often condemned, this type under the label of "the supernatural explained."

Let us take as an example of the fantastic-uncanny the same *Saragossa Manuscript.* All of the "miracles" are explained rationally at the end of the narrative. Alfonso meets in a cave the hermit who had sheltered him at the beginning, and who is the grand sheik of the Gomélez himself. This man reveals the machinery of all the foregoing events:

> Don Emmanuel de Sa, the Governor of Cadiz, is one of the initiates. He had sent you Lopez and Moschite, who abandoned you at the spring of Alcornoques. ... By means of a sleeping potion you were made to waken the next day under the gallows of the Zoto brothers. Whence you came to my hermitage, where you encountered the dreadful Pascheco, who is in fact a Basque dancer. ... The following day, you were subjected to a far crueler ordeal: the false inquisition which threatened you with horrible tortures but did not succeed in shaking your courage.

Doubt had been sustained up to this point, as we know, between two poles: the existence of the supernatural and a series of rational explanations. Let us now enumerate the types of explanation that erode the case for the supernatural: first, accident or coincidence—for in the supernatural world, instead of chance there prevails what we might call "pan-determinism" (an explanation in terms of chance is what works against the supernatural in "Inès de las Sierras"); next, dreams (a solution proposed in *Le Diable Amoureux); *then the influence of drugs (Alfonso's dreams during the first night); tricks and prearranged apparitions (an essential solution in *The Saragossa Manuscript): *illusion of the senses (we shall find examples of this in Théophile Gautier's "La Morte Amoureuse" and John Dickson Carr's *The Burning Court); *and lastly madness, as in Hoffmann's "Princess Brambilla." There are obviously two groups of "excuses" here which correspond to the oppositions real/ imaginary and real/illusory. In the first group, there has been no supernatural occurrence, for nothing at all has actually occurred; what we imagined we saw was only the fruit of a deranged imagination (dream, madness, the influence of drugs). In the second group, the events indeed occurred, but they may be explained rationally (as coincidences, tricks, illusions).

We recall that in the definitions of the fantastic cited above,[1] the rational solution was decided as "completely stripped of internal probability" (Solovyov) or as a loophole "small enough to be unusable" (M. R. James). Indeed, the realistic solutions given in *The Saragossa Manuscript* or "Inès de las Sierras" are altogether improbable; supernatural solutions would have been, on the contrary, quite probable. The coincidences are too artificial in Nodier's tale. As for *The Saragossa Manuscript,* its author does not even try to concoct a credible ending: the story of the treasure, of the hollow mountain, of the empire of the Gomélez is more incredible than that of the women transformed into corpses! The probable is therefore not necessarily opposed to the fantastic: the former is a category that deals with internal coherence, with submission to the genre; the *fantastic* refers to an ambiguous perception shared by the reader and one of the characters. Within the genre of the fantastic, it is *probable* that "fantastic" reactions will occur.

In addition to such cases as these, where we find ourselves in the uncanny rather in spite of ourselves—in order to explain the fantastic—there also exists the uncanny in the pure state. In works that belong to this genre, events are related which may be readily accounted for by the laws of reason, but which are, in one way or another, incredible, extraordinary, shocking, singular, disturbing or unexpected, and which thereby provoke in the character and in the reader a reaction similar to that which works of the fantastic have made familiar. The definition is, as we see, broad and vague, but so is the genre which it describes: the uncanny is not a clearly delimited genre, unlike the fantastic. More precisely,

[1]Todorov is referring back here to his previous chapter: "Definition of the Fantastic"—Ed.

it is limited on just one side, that of the fantastic; on the other, it dissolves into the general field of literature (Dostoievsky's novels, for example, may be included in the category of the uncanny). According to Freud, the sense of the uncanny is linked to the appearance of an image which originates in the childhood of the individual or the race (a hypothesis still to be verified; there is not an entire coincidence between Freud's use of the term and our own). The literature of horror in its pure state belongs to the uncanny—many examples from the stories of Ambrose Bierce could serve as examples here.

The uncanny realizes...only one of the conditions of the fantastic: the description of certain reactions, especially of fear. It is uniquely linked to the sentiments of the characters and not to a material event defying reason. (The marvelous, by way of contrast, may be characterized by the mere presence of supernatural events, without implicating the reaction they provoke in the characters.)

Poe's tale "The Fall of the House of Usher" is an instance of the uncanny bordering on the fantastic. The narrator of this tale arrives at the house one evening summoned by his friend Roderick Usher, who asks him to stay for a time. Usher is a hypersensitive, nervous creature who adores his sister, now seriously ill. When she dies some days later, the two friends, instead of burying her, leave her body in one of the vaults under the house. Several days pass. On a stormy night the two men are sitting in a room together, the narrator reading aloud an ancient tale of chivalry. The sounds that are described in the chronicle seem to correspond to the noises they hear in the house itself. At the end, Roderick Usher stands up and says, in a scarcely audible voice: "We have put her living in the tomb!" And, indeed, the door opens, the sister is seen standing on the threshold. Brother and sister rush into each other's arms, and fall dead. The narrator flees the house just in time to see it crumble into the environing tarn.

Here the uncanny has two sources. The first is constituted by two coincidences (there are as many of these as in a work of the *supernatural explained*). Although the resurrection of Usher's sister and the fall of the house after the death of its inhabitants may appear supernatural, Poe has not failed to supply quite rational explanations for both events. Of the house, he writes:

"Perhaps the eye of a scrutinizing observer might have discovered a barely perceptible fissure, which, extending from the roof of the building in front, made its way down the wall in a zig-zag direction, until it became lost in the sullen waters of the tarn." And of Lady Madeline: "Frequent although transient affections of a partially cataleptical character were the unusual diagnosis." Thus the supernatural explanation is merely suggested, and one need not accept it.

The other series of elements that provoke the sense of the uncanny is not linked to the fantastic but to what we might call "an experience of limits," which characterizes the whole of Poe's *oeuvre*. Indeed, Baudelaire wrote of Poe: "No man has more magically described the *exceptions* of human life and of nature." Likewise Dostoievsky: "He almost always chooses the most exceptional reality, puts his character in the most exceptional situation, on the external or psychological level. ..." (Poe, moreover, wrote a tale on this theme, a "meta-uncanny" tale entitled "The Angel of the Odd.") In "The Fall of the House of Usher," it is the extremely morbid condition of the brother and sister which disturbs the reader. In other tales, scenes of cruelty, delight in evil, and murder will provoke the same effect. The sentiment of the uncanny originates, then, in certain themes linked to more or less ancient taboos. If we grant that primal experience is constituted by transgression, we can accept Freud's theory as to the origin of the uncanny.

Thus the fantastic is ultimately excluded from "The Fall of the House of Usher." As a rule, we do not find the fantastic in Poe's works, in the strict sense, with the exception perhaps of "The Black Cat." His tales almost all derive their effect from the uncanny, and several from the marvelous. Yet Poe remains very close to the authors of the fantastic both in his themes and in the techniques that he applies.

We also know that Poe originated the detective story or murder mystery, and this relationship is not a matter of chance. It has often been remarked, moreover, that for the reading public, detective stories have in our time replaced ghost stories. Let us consider the nature of this relationship. The murder mystery, in which we try to discover the identity of the criminal, is constructed in the following manner: on the one hand there are

several easy solutions, initially tempting but turning out, one
after another, to be false; on the other, there is an entirely improbable solution disclosed only at the end and turning out to be
the only right one. Here we see what brings the detective story
close to the fantastic tale. Recalling Solovyov's and James's
definitions, we note that the fantastic narrative, too, involves two
solutions, one probable and supernatural, the other improbable
and rational. It suffices, therefore, that in the detective story
this second solution be so inaccessible as to "defy reason" for us
to accept the existence of the supernatural rather than to rest
with the absence of any explanation at all. A classical example of
this situation is Agatha Christie's *Ten Little Indians.* Ten characters are isolated on an island; they are told (by a recording) that
they will all die, punished for a crime which the law cannot
punish. The nature of each death, moreover, is described in the
counting-rhyme "Ten Little Indians." The doomed characters —
and the reader along with them — vainly try to discover who is
carrying out the successive executions. They are alone on the
island and dying one after another, each in a fashion announced
by the rhyme; down to the last one, who — and it is this that
arouses an aura of the supernatural — does not commit suicide but
is killed in his turn. No rational explanation seems possible, we
must admit the existence of invisible beings or spirits. Obviously
this hypothesis is not really necessary: the rational explanation
will be given. The murder mystery approaches the fantastic, but
it is also the contrary of the fantastic: in fantastic texts, we tend
to prefer the supernatural explanation; the detective story, once
it is over, leaves no doubt as to the absence of supernatural
events. This relationship, moreover, is valid only for a certain
type of detective story (the "sealed room") and a certain type of
uncanny narrative (the "supernatural explained"). Further, the
emphasis differs in the two genres: in the detective story, the
emphasis is placed on the solution to the mystery; in the texts
linked to the uncanny (as in the fantastic narrative), the emphasis
is on the reactions which this mystery provokes. This structural
proximity nonetheless produces a resemblance which we must
take into account.

An author who deserves a more extended scrutiny when we
deal with the relation between detective stories and fantastic tales
is John Dickson Carr. Among his books there is one in particular

which raises the problem in an exemplary fashion, *The Burning Court.* As in *Ten Little Indians,* we are confronted with an apparently insoluble problem: four men open a crypt in which a corpse had been placed a few days before; the crypt is empty, but it is not possible that anyone could have opened it in the meantime. Throughout the story, moreover, ghosts and supernatural phenomena are evoked. There is a witness to the crime that had taken place, and this witness asserts he has seen the murderess leave the victim's room, passing through the wall at a place where a door existed two hundred years earlier. Furthermore, one of the persons implicated in the case, a young woman, believes herself to be a witch, or more precisely, a poisoner (the murder was the result of poison) who belongs to a particular type of human beings, *the non-dead:* "Briefly, the non-dead are those persons — commonly women — who have been condemned to death for the crime of poisoning, and whose bodies have been burnt at the stake, whether alive or dead," we learn later on. While leafing through a manuscript he has received from the publishing house that he works for, Stevens, the young woman's husband, happens on a photograph whose caption reads: *Marie d' Aubray: Guillotined for Murder, 1861.* The text continues: "He was looking at a photograph of his own wife." How could this young woman, some seventy years later, be the same person as a famous nineteenth-century poisoner, guillotined into the bargain? Quite simply, according to Stevens' wife, who is ready to assume responsibility for the present murder. A series of further coincidences seems to confirm the presence of the supernatural. Finally, a detective arrives, and everything begins to be explained. The woman who had been seen passing through the wall was an optical illusion caused by a mirror. The corpse had not vanished after all, but was cunningly concealed. Young Marie Stevens had nothing in common with a long-dead poisoner, though an effort had been made to make her believe that she had. The entire supernatural atmosphere had been created by the murderer in order to confuse the case, to avert suspicion. The actual guilty parties are discovered, even if they are not successfully punished.

Then follows an epilogue, as a result of which *The Burning Court* emerges from the class of detective stories that simply evoke the supernatural, to join the ranks of the fantastic. We see Marie once again, in her house, thinking over the case; and the fantastic re-emerges. Marie asserts once again (to the reader) that she is indeed the poisoner, that the detective was in fact her friend (which is not untrue), and that he has provided the entire rational explanation in order to save her ("It was clever of him to pluck a physical explanation, a thing of sizes and dimensions and stone walls").

The world of the non-dead reclaims its rights, and the fantastic with it: we are thrown back on our hesitation as to which solution to choose. But it must be noted, finally, that we are less concerned here with a resemblance between two genres than with their synthesis.

If we move to the *other* side of that median line which we have called the fantastic, we find ourselves in the fantastic-marvelous, the class of narratives that are presented as fantastic and that end with an acceptance of the supernatural. These are the narratives closest to the pure fantastic, for the latter, by the very fact that it remains unexplained, unrationalized, suggests the existence of the supernatural. The frontier between the two will therefore be uncertain; nonetheless, the presence or absence of certain details will always allow us to decide.

Gautier's "La Morte Amoureuse" can serve as an example. This is the story of a monk (Romuald) who on the day of his ordination falls in love with the courtesan Clarimonde. After several fleeting encounters, Romuald attends Clarimonde's deathbed—whereupon she begins to appear in his dreams, dreams that have a strange property: instead of conforming to impressions of each passing day, they constitute a continuous narrative. In his dreams, Romuald no longer leads the austere life of a monk, but lives in Venice in continuous revelry. And at the same time he realizes that Clarimonde has been keeping herself alive by means of blood she sucks from him during the night....

Up to this point, all the events are susceptible of rational explanations. The explanations are largely furnished by the dreams themselves ("May God grant that it is a dream!" Romuald exclaims, in this resembling Alvaro in *Le Diable Amoureux*). Illusions of the senses furnish another plausible explanation. Thus: "One evening, strolling along the box-lined paths of my little garden, *I seemed to see* through the hedgerow a woman's shape..."; "For a moment *I thought* I saw her foot move..."; "*I do not know if this was an illusion or a reflection of the lamp, but it seemed* that the blood began to circulate once more beneath that lustreless pallor," etc. (italics mine). Finally, a series of events can be considered as simply uncanny and due to chance. But Romuald himself is ready to regard the matter as a diabolic intervention:

> The strangeness of the episode. Clairmonde's supernatural [!] beauty, the phosphorescent lustre of her eyes, the burning touch of her hand, the confusion into which she had thrown me, the sudden change that had occurred in me—all of this clearly proved the presence of the Devil; and that silken hand was perhaps nothing but the glove in which he had clad his talons.

It might be the Devil, indeed, but it might also be chance and no more than that. We remain, then, up to this point in the fantastic in its pure state. At this moment there occurs an event which causes the narrative to swerve. Another monk, Sérapion, learns (we do not know how) of Romuald's adventure. He leads the latter to the graveyard in which Clarimonde lies buried, unearths the coffin, opens it, and Clarimonde appears, looking just as she did on the day of her death, a drop of blood on her lips. ... Seized by pious rage, Abbé Sérapion flings holy water on the corpse. "The wretched Clarimonde had no sooner been touched by the holy dew than her lovely body turned to dust; nothing was left but a shapeless mass of ashes and half-consumed bones." This entire scene, and in particular the metamorphosis of the corpse, cannot be explained by the laws of nature as they are generally acknowledged. We are here in the realm of the fantastic-marvelous.

A similar example is to be found in Villiers de l'Isle-Adam's "Véra." Here again, throughout the tale, we may hesitate between believing in life-after-death or thinking that the count who so believes is mad. But at the end, the count discovers the key to Véra's tomb in his own room, though he himself had flung it into the grave; it must therefore be Véra, his dead wife, who has brought it to him.

There exists, finally, a form of the marvelous in the pure state which—just as in the case of the uncanny in the pure state—has no distinct frontiers. ...In the case of the marvelous, supernatural elements provoke no particular reaction in either the characters or in the implicit reader. It is not an attitude toward the events described which characterizes the marvelous, but the nature of these events.

We note, in passing, how arbitrary the old distinction was between form and content: the event, which traditionally belonged to "content," here becomes a "formal" element. The converse is also true: the stylistic (hence "formal") procedure of modalization can have, as we have seen in connection with *Aurélia,* a precise content.

We generally link the genre of the marvelous to that of the fairy tale. But as a matter of fact, the fairy tale is only one of the varieties of the marvelous, and the supernatural events in fairy tales provoke no surprise: neither a hundred years' sleep, nor a talking wolf, nor the magical gifts of the fairies (to cite only a few elements in Perrault's tales). What distinguishes the fairy tale is a certain kind of writing, not the status of the supernatural. Hoffman's tales illustrate this difference perfectly: "The Nutcracker and the Mouse-King," "The Strange Child," and "The King's Bride" belong, by stylistic properties, to the fairy tale. "The Choice of a Bride," while preserving the same status with regard to the supernatural, is not a fairy tale at all. One would also have to characterize the *Arabian Nights* as marvelous tales rather than fairy tales (a subject which deserves a special study all its own).

In order to delimit the marvelous in the pure state, it is convenient to isolate it from several types of narrative in which the supernatural is somewhat justified.

1. We may speak first of all of *hyperbolic marvelous*. In it, phenomena are supernatural only by virtue of their dimensions, which are superior to those that are familiar to us. Thus in the *Arabian Nights* Sinbad the Sailor declares he has seen "fish one hundred and even two hundred ells long" or "serpents so great and so long that there was not one which could not have swallowed an elephant." But perhaps this is no more than a simple manner of speaking (we shall study this question when we deal with the poetic or allegorical interpretation of the text); one might even say, adapting a proverb, that "fear has big eyes." In any case, this form of the supernatural does not do excessive violence to reason.

2. Quite close to this first type of the marvelous is the *exotic marvelous*. In this type, supernatural events are reported without being presented as such. The implicit reader is supposed to be ignorant of the regions where the events take place, and consequently he has no reason for calling them into question. Sinbad's second voyage furnishes some excellent examples, such as the *roc*, a bird so tremendous that it concealed the sun and "one of whose legs...was as great as a great tree-trunk." Of course, this bird does not exist for contemporary zoology, but Sinbad's hearers were far from any such certainty and, five centuries later, Galland himself writes: "Marco Polo, in his travels, and Father Martini, in his *History of China,* speaks of this bird," etc. A little later, Sinbad similarly describes the rhinoceros, which however is well known to us:

> There is, on the same island, a rhinoceros, a creature smaller than the elephant and larger than the buffalo: it bears a single horn upon its snout, about one ell long; this horn is solid and severed through the center, from one end to the other. Upon it may be seen white lines which represent the face of a man. The rhinoceros attacks the elephant, pierces it with its horn through the belly, carries it off and bears it upon its head; but when the elephant's blood flows over its eyes and blinds it, the rhinoceros falls to the ground, and—what will amaze you [indeed], the roc comes and bears off both creatures in its talons, in order to feed its young upon their bodies.

This virtuoso passage shows, by its mixture of natural and supernatural elements, the special character of the *exotic marvelous.* The mixture exists, of course, only for the modern reader; the narrator implicit in the tale situates everything on the same level (that of the "natural").

3. A third type of the marvelous might be called the *instrumental marvelous.* Here we find the gadgets, technological developments unrealized in the period described but, after all, quite possible. In the "Tale of Prince Ahmed" in the *Arabian Nights,* for instance, the marvelous instruments are, at the beginning: a flying carpet, an apple that cures diseases, and a "pipe" for seeing great distances; today, the helicopter, antibiotics, and binoculars, endowed with the same qualities, do not belong in any way to the marvelous. The same is true of the flying horse in the "Tale of the

Magic Horse." Similarly in the case of the revolving stone in the "Tale of Ali Baba," we need only think of recent espionage films in which a safe opens only when its owner's voice utters certain words. We must distinguish these objects, products of human skill, from certain instruments that are often similar in appearance but whose origin is magical, and that serve to communicate with other worlds. Thus Aladdin's lamp and ring, or the horse in "The Third Calender's Tale," which belong to a different kind of marvelous.

4. The "instrumental marvelous" brings us very close to what in nineteenth-century France was called the *scientific marvelous*, which today we call *science fiction*. Here the supernatural is explained in a rational manner, but according to laws which contemporary science does not acknowledge. In the high period of fantastic narratives, stories involving magnetism are characteristic of the scientific marvelous: magnetism "scientifically" explains supernatural events, yet magnetism itself belongs to the supernatural. Examples are Hoffmann's "Spectre Bridegroom" or "The Magnetizer," and Poe's "The Facts in the Case of M. Valdemar" or Maupassant's "Un Fou?" Contemporary science fiction, when it does not slip into allegory, obeys the same mechanism: these narratives, starting from irrational premises, link the "facts" they contain in a perfectly logical manner. ...

All these varieties of the marvelous—"excused," justified, and imperfect—stand in opposition to the marvelous in its pure—unexplained—state. We shall not consider it here...because the aspiration to the marvelous, as an anthropological phenomenon, exceeds the context of a study limited to literary aspects. In any case, the marvelous has been, from this perspective, the object of several penetrating books; and in conclusion, I shall borrow from one of these, Pierre Mabille's *Miroir du Merveilleux*, a sentence which neatly defines the meaning of the marvelous:

> Beyond entertainment, beyond curiosity, beyond all the emotions such narratives and legends afford, beyond the need to divert, to forget, or to achieve delightful or terrifying sensations, the real goal of the marvelous journey is the total exploration of universal reality.

A Dark Romanticism:
In Quest of a Gothic Monomyth

by G. R. Thompson

In art history the word *Gothic* normally refers to various architectural styles of cathedrals built during the Middle Ages. In literature the word refers to the kind of work, usually fiction, that developed during the later eighteenth and earlier nineteenth centuries out of the sentimental romance into the Dark Romantic tale of terror. The word *Romantic* usually evokes an ideal world, infused with internal energy and dynamically evolving toward a yet higher state, in which the single, separate self seeks unity with Nature, itself symbolic of the aesthetic harmony of the cosmos. Adding the adjective *Dark* may evoke an image of the lonely, isolated self, pressing onward despite all obstacles while either indulging or struggling with an internal evil, the very conflict a source of energy. But when the word *Gothic* is applied to literature, it merely evokes images of ghosts, demons, trapdoors, castles. In America, Gothic fiction is frequently associated with the "dime novel," in Britain perhaps more precisely called the "shilling-shocker" or the "penny-dreadful." All three terms point to the origins of the Gothic romance as a popular literature, inexpensively produced for a mass audience, with the consequent implication that it is merely a literature of surfaces and sensations.

This judgment tends to ameliorate somewhat when the osten-

sible genre of such literature is poetry or drama. In poetry, one
has to contend with the names of Byron, Coleridge, and Keats;
and in drama, one thinks immediately of the bloody revenge
plays of Shakespeare and Webster, replete with ghosts and visions.
Certain masterworks of Gothic fiction have been acknowledged
— *The Monk, Melmoth the Wanderer, Frankenstein*—but the
suspicion persists that these are lesser works than the "standard"
classics. And classic works of fiction which employ Gothic conventions and subjects, like *Heart of Darkness,* tend not to be
critically examined in the tradition of a developing Gothic mode
but in some other, more acceptable tradition of the novel. Thus,
although critics will grant that a work like *Wuthering Heights*
comes out of the Gothic tradition, it is usually regarded as
transcending its surface mode of Gothic. The prime example of
this critical phenomenon, perhaps, is *Moby-Dick,* for it has
seemed to most readers somehow reductive to call Melville's
novel a Gothic romance. Yet its very Gothic quality may be what
gives such a wild and whirling work as *Moby-Dick* its peculiar
excellence.

Indeed, in France the Gothic has long been considered a *genre,*
though the French meaning of the word may differ slightly from
the English. But a theory of *genre* that precisely defines, analyzes,
and distinguishes among themes, subject matters, formal elements, characteristic devices, philosophical concerns, or a developing tradition is yet to be written. The twentieth-century
assumption of the essential rightness of dividing literary genres
into fiction, poetry, drama, biography, and essay is obviously
inadequate for a history of literature. At one time, the principal
genres were—in view of what had been written—epic, tragic, and
lyric—established forms we still recognize but the precise de-
limitations of which dissolve the closer we examine them. We
have had Henry Fielding's "comic epic in prose," as well as tragic
drama, tragic poetry, prose tragedy, lyric drama, dramatic lyrics,
and so on; and one may recall Polonius' reading of the players'
list of types in *Hamlet:* "...tragedy, comedy, history, pastoral,
pastoral-comical, historical-pastoral, tragical-historical, tragical-
comical-historical-pastoral, scene individable or poem un-
limited." The question therefore becomes one of recurrent con-

figurations of concerns, themes, subjects, characters, conflicts, conventions, modes, devices, or images that identify the Gothic as a form. Such a question does not necessarily imply an exclusive differentiation from all other genres. *Moby-Dick,* again, is part narrative, part drama, part poetry, part essay. It is also deeply Gothic throughout. ...

[In examining] the darker side of Romanticism...the parameters of a Dark Romantic genre [begin] to outline themselves. ... What emerges is an essay toward a definition of the Gothic in literature—an exploration, however tentative, in quest of a Gothic monomyth that explains the curious power of the literature—something beyond the local terrors and horrors of stage villains and trembling heroines and ghostly manifestations. ... The kind of high Gothic represented by *Melmoth,* or *Moby-Dick,* or *Heart of Darkness* is the embodiment of demonic-quest romance, in which a lonely, self-divided hero embarks on insane pursuit of the Absolute. This self-destructive quest is metaphysical, mythic, and religious, defining the hero's dark or equivocal relationship to the universe. Its imagery characteristically employs an iconography tracing an unbroken tradition to the Age of Faith. ...

The concept of the icon, both verbal and visual, is an important means of illustrating the extent of the continuity of Medieval Gothic and Romantic Gothic, bringing graphic proof to religious claims and religious significance to formalist observations. Medieval images and motifs are used by later writers to define a negative or positive relationship to God. ... The Romantic [Age was fascinated] with the duality of the Middle Ages. This duality finds expression, on the one hand, in the evocation of the transcendent, upward thrust of Gothic cathedrals and in the "romances" of idealized knights in quest of the Holy Grail; and, on the other hand, in the vision of the dark night of the soul and the nightmare terror of demons Satan sent from Hell to drag man down. Romantic Gothic deals with the tormented condition of a creature suspended between the extremes of faith and skepticism, beatitude and horror, being and nothingness, love and hate—and anguished by an indefinable guilt for some crime it cannot remember having committed.

As the foregoing suggests, the phrase "tale of terror" is inadequate to describe the effect of the Gothic romance, for it has a complex rather than a single unified impact — Poe's famous definitions notwithstanding. The chief element of the Gothic romance is not so much terror as, more broadly, dread — whether physical, psychological, or metaphysical, whether of body, mind, or spirit. The Gothic romance seeks to create an atmosphere of dread by combining terror with horror and mystery. *Terror* suggests the frenzy of physical and mental fear of pain, dismemberment, and death. *Horror* suggests the perception of something incredibly evil or morally repellent. *Mystery* suggests something beyond this, the perception of a world that stretches away beyond the range of human intelligence — often morally incomprehensible — and thereby productive of a nameless apprehension that may be called religious dread in the face of the wholly *other*. When in Gothic literature this sense of mystery is joined with terror or horror, the effects of each expand beyond ordinary fear or repugnance. Mrs. Radcliffe suggested as much in her often-misunderstood essay "On the Supernatural in Poetry," wherein she asserts that terror and horror are really "opposite." Terror "expands the soul" and "wakens the faculties to a high degree"; horror "contracts, freezes, and nearly annihilates them." But this is another paradox of Gothic duality; terror and horror represent complementary poles of a single continuum of perception and response. Terror, in her terms, may be seen as coming upon us from without, engulfing us with an aweful sense of the sublime in which sense of self is swallowed in immensity — whereas horror rises up from within, with a vague consciousness of the "dreader evil" sinking downward through levels of subconscious "uncertainty and obscurity" into a vast unconscious reservoir of primitive dread. The central image for these paradoxes in the Gothic is the cathedral itself, for it has both an outward, upward movement toward the heavens, and an inward, downward motion, convoluting in upon itself in labyrinthine passages and dark recesses, descending to catacombs deep in the earth.

But while we conceive of the Gothic romance as evoking that supernatural sense of mystery associated with the dark interior of a cathedral, the earliest meanings of the English word *Gothic* involved an elementary kind of aesthetic and cultural disapproval based on imprecise historical hypotheses. Early eighteenth-century writers used *Gothic* to indicate any architectural structure not in the "classical" style of Greece and Rome; they hypothesized that "Gothic" or other northern barbarians had invaded the Roman empire, wreaking destruction on the true art of the ancient Roman works and replacing them with a "fantastical" manner of building characterized by walls that were too thick, towers that were too tall, arches that were too steeply pointed. This unhappy circumstance was made yet more lamentable in their eyes by subsequent infusions of Arab temple styles during the Moorish invasions of Europe between the twelfth and thirteenth centuries. The effect of such structures on the human mind, they thought, was a barbarous "confusion." In retrospect, however, this eighteenth-century response can be seen as reflective of the consistent duality found also in the Gothic literature of the end of the century: on the one hand, the sublime evoked the thrill of mystery and wonder, the aspiration upward toward God; on the other hand, it evoked a ponderous, depressing sense of somber gloom, as well as terror engendered by such demonic ornamentation as bass figures and gargoyles within and without the cathedral. In 1764-65, Horace Walpole in *The Castle of Otranto,* usually considered the first Gothic romance in English, emphasized the vaults, stained windows, tombs, darkness, and carefully coordinated perspective of Medieval buildings—a perspective that in the cathedral was designed to bring the observer to his knees. Walpole's work effected a shift of meaning in the most common use of the word *Gothic* from the architectural denotation of "Medieval buildings" to the emotional effect of weird, supernatural, fantastic, and terrifying events in a work of literature in which the Medieval cathedral or castle served as a theater for such events.

Between 1750 and 1800, however, a larger reevaluation of the Gothic emphasized the "natural" symbology that man-made cathedrals presented. Edmund Burke in his *Enquiry into the Sublime and Beautiful* (1756-57) observed that a certain "wildness" in nature and art produced the effect of the "sublime" through the evocation of a sense of supernatural mystery. Others observed that the external mass of the cathedral suggested a mountain and that the interior, profuse with grotesque scroll-

work around windows and ceilings, suggested branches and
groves of trees. By the turn of the century German Romantic
writers were contending that Gothic buildings were actually
symbols of forests, icons of the primitive, natural, Edenic habitat
of man. And by 1825, British and American Romanticists had in-
verted the equation, as articulated in William Cullen Bryant's
"A Forest Hymn":

> The groves were God's first temples. Ere man learned
> To hew the shaft, and lay the architrave,
> And spread the roof above them—ere he framed
> The lofty vault, to gather and roll back
> The sound of anthems; in the darkling wood,
> Amid the cool and silence, he knelt down. ...

Here we have an expression of a view adopted by many
European and American writers of the later eighteenth and
earlier nineteenth centuries—namely, transcendental, cosmic
optimism—that spiritual and aesthetic faith in a harmoniously
integrated, organic universe dynamically evolving toward a yet
higher and better state. The overt cultural values of the earlier
nineteenth century in Europe and America were, of course,
solidly Christian, Enlightenment losses of faith notwithstanding.
In one sense, the cosmic optimism of Romantic thinkers was the
secularization of a powerful Christian tradition and liturgy into
a rhetoric that ostensibly omitted an anthropomorphized God
but which still assumed a deific force. This God-force seemed to
be dynamically propelling man through a prefigured (though not
precisely predestined) pattern of events toward some beneficent
end; and the element of God's justified vengeance and wrath
upon sinful and fallen man that formed one aspect of Medieval
Christian thought was temporarily submerged in the dominance
of this optimistic Romanticism. But the apprehension that there
was a dark substratum to the rock of Romantic faith obsessed those
Romantic writers who turned to the Gothic mode of terror and
horror in an effort to express a complex vision of the existential
agony confronting man since the Age of Faith.

Fallen man's inability fully to comprehend haunting reminders
of another, supernatural realm that yet seemed not to exist, the
constant perplexity of inexplicable and vastly metaphysical
phenomena, a propensity for seemingly perverse or evil moral

choices that had no firm or fixed measure or rule, and a sense of nameless guilt combined with a suspicion that the external world was a delusive projection of the mind—these were major elements in the vision of man that the Dark Romantics opposed to the mainstream of Romantic thought. This vision was reenforced by the recently propounded subjective philosophies of Berkeley, Hume, and Kant in the second half of the eighteenth century. And once the doubt was established in the Dark Romantic mind, it did not matter whether one assumed the world to be objective or subjective, for the same dialectics of agony could apply to either. If one contemplates the world as object, it may be either a structure infused with spirit and supplying neoplatonic symbols of the other dynamic life beyond this one, or mere physical material with no object beyond the immediate fact of existence. If one contemplates the world as subject, then it may either be a dynamic projection of the indwelling spirit of man himself, or a deceptive, arbitrary imposition of idiosyncratic meaning upon Void. Moreover, Medieval antecedents clearly conceive of Void as double. The Void of Plenitude asserted God's immanence in all things; the Void of Nothingness imaged God's absence. The Dark Romantics tended toward an ambiguous mid-region of agonized doubt or suspension, believing neither in Plenitude nor in Nothingness—though obsessed with the latter possibility.

In a Romantic context, then; Gothic literature may be seen as expressive of an existential terror generated by a schism between a triumphantly secularized philosophy of evolving good and an abiding obsession with the Medieval conception of guilt-laden, sin-ridden man. In part, Gothic themes represent a quest for a theory adequate to world perceived as mind. In the absence of any satisfactory theory that accounted for the existence of evil and pain, the Gothic tale could at least embody the world felt, if not perceived, as mind. If Romanticism is largely a philosophy of consciousness, Dark Romanticism is the drama of the mind engaged in the quest for metaphysical and moral absolutes in a world that offers shadowy semblances of an occult order but withholds final revelation and illumination. If a distinction between the Romantic Gothic imagination and the Dark Romantic imagination can be made, it is perhaps that the purely Gothic vision ends in despair, pain, and annihilation. The Gothic hero is ulti-

mately torn apart by demons. The Dark Romantic hero, by work-
ing in and through evil and darkness, by withholding final in-
vestment of belief in either good or evil, by enduring the
treachery of his own mind, and by accepting his crucifixion by
whatever demonic forces may exist, perhaps attains some
Sisyphean or Promethean semblance of victory.

In any event, as dramas of darkness, the literary productions
of the Romantic Gothic mind embody this nameless dread in
characters of flesh and blood. Whereas transcendental Romantic
thought attempted in essence to depersonalize or de-anthropo-
morphize the traditional Void of Plenitude, in which the God-
spirit was imminent but not particularized, the Dark Romantics
adapted images of anthropomorphized evil in the form of Satan,
devils, ghosts, lamia, incubi, succubi, vampires, and ghouls.
While these demonic creatures frequently inhabit an ambiguous
landscape of duplicitous imagery, the recurrent images in the
literature of terror and horror are yet vivid. The empty seascapes,
frozen wastes, bottomless abysses, vast blank landscapes are opposed to images of aspirational height in cathedral vaulting or
spires; darkness is opposed to luminous shining forth; a solitary
figure edging toward the precipice, surrounded by forked
lightning threatening to blast his wracked body, is opposed to
the resurrection of the body in full perfection of form, surrounded
by the ascending heavenly host. In addition to symbolizing the
particular dramatic situation, however, Romantic Gothic imagery
employs a rich complex of traditional images—in short a Christian
iconography of fallen man. But the difference is that in Romantic
Gothic literature man is confronted with an ambiguous world
structure rather than the clearcut world of the Middle Ages. Instead, he faces a world that he has no hope of comprehending and
in which he cannot make the proper moral choices, even though
he is yet held responsible by some occult power for such choices.

Now, by an "iconography" of the Gothic, or more broadly of
Dark Romanticism, we should understand several things simultaneously about the literature: the obsessive images and recurring
emblematic figures; the recurring religious undercurrent of
meaning; and some sort of objective correlative found both in
specific works and in the "genre" that co-relates the themes of
physical terror, moral horror, and religious mystery with recur-

ring character types and recurring images of desolate landscapes and seascapes, castles and cathedrals, towers and dungeons. As suggested, in a large sense, we are in quest of a Gothic monomyth; but more specifically we are in quest of a verbal icon that brings together the various threads and strands of the Gothic fabric. Here, of course, I borrow a phrase from W. K. Wimsatt's *The Verbal Icon*. In this volume, addressing himself to a theory of verbal meaning, Wimsatt deals with the "interpenetration of abstractly stated meaning and the more concrete, unspecified, and diffusive meaning of metaphors and dramatic structures." In the epigraph to the book as a whole, Wimsatt defines this construct as follows:

> The term *icon* is used today by semeiotic writers to refer to a verbal sign which *somehow* shares the properties of, or resembles, the objects which it denotes. The same term in its more usual meaning refers to a visual image and especially to one which is a religious symbol. The verbal image which most fully realizes its verbal capacities is that which is not merely a bright picture (in the usual modern meaning of the term *image*) but also an interpretation of reality in its metaphoric and symbolic dimensions.

...Gothic writers [persist] in using religious symbols and images as a vehicle for presenting a picture of man as eternal victim—victim of both himself and of something outside himself. The demons, gods, mythic heroes, and other human icons, along with castle, cathedral, manor house, temple, graveyard, churchyard, charnel house, dungeon, labyrinth, cave, icebound seas, high mountain crags, lightning, storms—are all, simultaneously, emblems of supernatural power external to the human mind, and of the agony within the human mind and spirit. They are metaphors of the self and of the nameless other, conjoined for a metaphor of the agonizing duality imbedded deep in the human personality.

Quest of the Numinous:
The Gothic Flame

by Devendra P. Varma

...During the earlier decades of the eighteenth century a stiff and starched formality had been more and more definitely imposed upon both poetry and prose. Those influences which had taught a flamboyant but none the less untidy literature a certain decorum and restraint, had in their turn become paralysed in a deathlike rigour. The Gothic novel was a symptom of general reaction against the forces of an exhausted Augustanism, and part of the movement which relaxed the classical restraints and widened the range of human sympathies, inciting literary minds to original, creative activity. Occasionally tinged with whimsicality and passion, often chaotic yet full of wonders, these novels are a key to the imaginative vision of a thrilling world and the exciting revelations of the unconscious. Immensely stimulating to the cramped fancy of the age, these fictions alone were strong enough to break the limitations of polished intellectual poetry and restore the fanciful, the terrible, and the sublime.

The rise of the Gothic novel may be connected with depravity, and a decline of religion. The sense of guilt, psychologists tell us, is deeply rooted in man, and when a religion loses its hold upon men's hearts, they must find some other outlet for their sense of guilt. It may be that the Gothic novelist experienced a sort of catharsis or mithridatic purging of his fears and self-questionings in the portrayal of horrors which proceeded from the frenzy of the creative brain, and perhaps comforted himself by suggesting that life is a mystery which death solves, and whose horrors fade away as a tale that is told. Perhaps his animal faculties of fear and inquisitiveness demanded a vent. But undoubtedly the Gothic romances were never born out of pure perversity, nor were they the mere titillation of jaded senses.

It remains to ascertain why horror so forcibly invaded literature just at this period. The late seventeenth and early eighteenth centuries have been recognized as, in all essentials, dominated by a strict concept of reason, that banished the emotional aura of religion and reduced the Deity to a clockwork Prime Mover of the Universe. The late eighteenth and early nineteenth centuries saw a new recognition of the heart's emotions and a reassertion of the numinous. It was these factors that produced the "Gothic" horror. Like Love, Horror is an individual, primal emotion; and it was a revival of pure emotion that these authors essayed within the isolated framework of the frowning castle and smiling meadow, with plots designed solely for emotional effect. Their hankering for emotion after an ultra-reasonable age demanded the crudest, most violently contrasted expression: it resembles the exaggerated, spontaneous reaction of children to the horror of the obscure and inexplicable, to giants and goblins.

In particular, these novels indicate a new, tentative apprehension of the Divine. Monastic life was no longer believed in, but at least it recalled the Ages of Faith and the alluring mystery of their discipline. The ghosts and demons, the grotesque manifestations of the supernatural, aroused the emotions by which man had first discovered his soul and realized the presence of a Being greater far than he, one who created and destroyed at will. Man's first stirring of religious instinct was his acute horror of this powerful Deity—and it was to such primitive emotion that he reverted, emancipated from reason, but once again ignorant of God, his spiritual world in chaos.

Primarily the Gothic novels arose out of a quest for the numinous. They are characterized by an awestruck apprehension of Divine immanence penetrating diurnal reality. This sense of the numinous is an almost archetypal impulse inherited from primitive magic. The Gothic quest was not merely after horror—a simple succession of ghastly incidents could have satisfied that yearning—but after other-worldly gratification. These novelists were seeking a *"frisson nouveau,"* a *"frisson"* of the supernatural.

They were moving away from the arid glare of rationalism towards the beckoning shadows of a more intimate and mystical interpretation of life, and this they encountered in the profound sense of the numinous stamped upon the architecture, paintings, and fable of the Middle Ages. The consequent "renaissance of wonder" created a world of imaginative conjurings in which the Divine was not a theorem but a mystery filled with dread. The phantoms that prowl along the corridors of the haunted castle would have no more power to awe than the rats behind fluttering tapestries, did they not bear token of a realm that is revealed only to man's mystical apperception, his source of all absolute spiritual values.

Supernatural manifestations have the power to fascinate and appal, for they touch the secret springs of mortal apprehension which connects our earthly with our spiritual being. Superstitions like the appearance of the dead among the living are perhaps most touching, since they excite a cold and shuddering sympathy for the strange beings whom we may ourselves resemble in a few short years. They are mute witnesses of our alliance with a greater power and make us aware of our fleshly infirmity and our higher destiny. As we listen with a tremulous eagerness to the echoes from beyond the grave, our curiosity and awe assume the immensity of passions. As Schopenhauer said, men are mere phantoms and dream pictures; "golden dreams hover over our cradle, and shadows thicken round the natural descent of the aged into the grave." All that appears real about us is but the thinnest shadow of a dream: in Nietzsche's words, "underneath this reality in which we live and have our being, another and altogether different reality lies concealed."

Man's spirit therefore feeds on mystery, and his soul is quickened by the icy touch of fear, for he experiences pure terror only when confronted by the dim, indestructible world of the supernatural. The quiverings of spirit which are base when prompted by things sordid and earthly, become sublime when inspired by a sense of the visionary and immortal. The Gothic novelists strike a union between our spiritual curiosities and venial terrors, and mediate between the world without us and the world within us; they make external nature redolent of noble associations and clothe the affections of the human heart with a spiritual dignity.

The spirit world is not the illusion of a dreaming brain; feelings of belief in life after death give energy to virtue and stability to principle. These novels enable us to comprehend, perhaps, the sublimity of that Deity who first called us into being, and thus elevate us above the evils of this world by granting us the sense of being the centre of powers more than earthly. The Gothic novel appeals to the night-side of the soul. As we close its pages we shudder at the horrifying tales of Satanic spirits and accursed beings, of mortals endowed with diabolical powers, and we recognize the evils of the soul that they represent. All the main "gothic" characters share the unreality and eeriness of ghosts. The same "otherworldliness," the same terrifying aloofness from common mortality exhales from Mary Shelley's "Monster" and the Wandering Jew of the Ahasuerus legend.

The authors of these works stand in the same relation to the reality of dreams as the philosopher to the reality of existence. We discover our larger life in dreams, and the Gothic novel lifts us from the narrow rut and enables us to join the unspaced firmament; it adds eternity to our trivial hours; and gives a sense of infinity to our finite existence. In short, it evokes in us the same feelings that the Gothic cathedrals evoked in medieval man.

"Beneath the multifarious crotchets and pinnacles, with which the Gothic novelists adorned his fictional fantasies, lay certain general principles of structure," says Michael Sadleir. In texture and design these novels echo the intricate workmanship of Gothic cathedrals. These authors build their tales around suggestive hints and dim pictures; their pastoral scenes and complicated adventures are deftly related to the final catastrophe. Their masterly ordering of incidents, their contribution to the structure of the novel as an art form, is distinctive and impressive. The Gothic novel was not a cul-de-sac, but an important arterial development of the novel.

These novelists were the first to perceive and emphasize the dramatic method which has since become a platitude of narrative theory. Their methods and technique inspired Scott's feelings for individual scenes, led to the use of dramatic methods by Victorian novelists, the use of suspense in short stories by Poe and his successors, and eventually the mystifications and solutions of the modern detective novels and thrillers.

To bring the supernatural palpably into a scene, requires a

bold experiment on the part of the novelist, and necessitates a long note of preparation and a whole train of circumstances that may gradually and insensibly lull the mind to an implicit credence. A series of incidents alone is, however, not enough to evoke terror; these have to make a strong impression on the mind. The Gothic novelist knew the potentialities of his art, and achieved his effects by one of two methods: the realistic or the poetic. The first attempted to produce a semblance of fact by means of detailed description or by pretence to a logical sequence of reasoning; the second aimed at arousing a poetic faith of the kind that Coleridge called "a willing suspension of disbelief." The Gothic novelists adopted either or both methods and reinforced effects by skillfully and powerfully agitating the reader's feelings. ...

The artistic manipulation of suspense in the Gothic tales developed along various lines. First we meet with "the black veil" method of Mrs. Radcliffe: Emily in *The Mysteries of Udolpho* quivers in front of a dark velvet pall which uncannily sways in the noctural wind. She draws aside the veil to confront a hideous corpse, putrid and dropping to decay. Again in the chamber of the dead Marchioness she shivers before the inky curtains, and perceives the folds moving unaccountably, when suddenly a repulsive face peers out at her. Inexplicable music forms another common device for creating suspense. Mysterious disappearances likewise increase the tension. Lights that glimmer and fade away, doors which open and close without any mortal aid, and groans and wails of unexplained origin heighten the effect. Dread secrets half-revealed at the hour of death, and mysterious manuscripts half-deciphered in failing light, likewise stimulate intense curiosity. ...

Indirectly, by tracing in fiction the progress and consequence of one strong, indulged passion, another trait adopted from the drama, [the Gothic novel] gave an impetus towards that science of psychology which was to turn into a craze and fashion a hundred years hence. They forecast the technique of the future novel by presenting certain subtle studies of character-physiognomy. Thus, by portraying mental states and emotions of characters, they enlarged the scope of the novel, and by sounding the whole gamut of fear, pointed towards the psychological novel of over a century later.

The Gothic villains are a prime example of their creator's instinctive feeling for psychologically interesting characters who yet merge with the pervading theme of the supernatural. We can distinguish three types of Gothic villain: the character of Manfred fashioned by Walpole in 1764, a type composed of ambitious tyranny and unbridled passion, who developed through Lord Lovel of Clara Reeve's *The Old English Baron;* the early villains of Mrs. Radcliffe, culminating in Count Montorio of Maturin and the character of Guzman in *Melmoth the Wanderer,* and also another descended from *Karl Moor,* the chieftain of Schiller's *Robbers* (1781). The latter type presents an "imposing figure." He is an outlaw, a Rousseauistic sentimentalist, a humanitarian who combats life's injustices, follies, and hypocrisies. Haunted by a sense of loneliness, helplessness, and despair, similar Victims of Destiny are La Motte in *The Romance of the Forest,* Falkland in *Caleb Williams,* and in *St. Leon,* the disfigured, misanthropic outlaw captain.

The third type of Gothic villain is the terrible "superman" whose ways lie in darkness and whose strength originates far beyond mortal thought. He is a new mintage of the Satan portrayed by Milton in *Paradise Lost*—the immortal outcast, a masterful, vaunting villain, his spirit unbroken even in defeat. He is the Rosicrucian, the Alchemist staking his very life on some dark hope, and behind him is all the mystery of Cabbala, Freemasonry, Medieval Satanism. This Miltonic superman appears in these novels for the first time in *Eblis,* ruler of the realm of despair in Beckford's *Vathek* (1786). Nine years later Lewis introduced Lucifer in *The Monk.* Schemoli, the villainous monk of Maturin's *Family of Montorio* (1807) is obviously modelled upon his formidable predecessor Schedoni, Mrs. Radcliffe's physical superman endowed with a ruined aristocratic past and mysterious intellectual power.

These three main types have been presented in order of increasing complexity. Manfred, a kind of wicked baron born out of fairy-tale, becomes the Victim of Destiny, a supersensitive being drawn to evil against his better will, impelled by blind Fate; a character who sentimentalizes over bygone days. The superman combines the qualities of both—Manfred assumes a gigantic physique and overwhelming motive, and the Victim of Destiny is now presented as the victim of injustice. Like Satan or the Ghost-Seer he has tempted fate, or has a Faustian compact imposed on him like the Wandering Jew. Paying an outrageous price for enormous benefits, he usurps his powers, then wraps his suffering in proud and lonely gloom. These three main types are fluid concepts which continually interact, though not annihilating distinction, for the Gothic villain remains to the last not a bundle of characteristics, but a set of characters. For the most part he is all melodrama and extravagant emotion, designed to excite the last possible twinge of sensation. His gradual development illustrates increasing skill in the art of romance. In him we see also the emergence of the "Romantic" character—an alien soul solacing itself in occult experiments with forbidden sciences or unscrupulous deeds. Lastly, the Gothic villain, like Frankenstein's monster, destroyed its creator, the Gothic novel.

Interpreted in its social context, the Gothic novel is a subtle and complex aesthetic expression of the spirit of Europe in revolutionary ferment. It is the most characteristic literary expression of the orgy of mental and emotional excitement that accompanied the French Revolution and grew out of the Industrialization of Britain. Since it is an expression of the late eighteenth-century *zeitgeist,* aspiring towards a more individual, spiritual world, an examination of it illuminates certain important aspects of the period.

The "fantastic" in literature is the surrealistic expression of those historical and social factors which the ordinary chronicle of events in history does not consider significant. Such "fantasia" express the profoundest, repressed emotions of the individual and society. John Draper has observed that "the existence or the lack of social tranquillity...governs both the amount of literature producible and the types of literature produced."

The Marquis de Sade, in his preface to *Les Crimes de l'Amour* (1800), expressed the following opinion on the Gothic novel: "Then there are the new novels, nearly whose whole merit lies in magic and phantasmagoria, with the *Monk* at their head, which are not entirely without merit; they are the fruit of the revolution of which all Europe felt the shock." André Breton considers the Gothic novels pathognominic of the social turmoils which agitated the whole of Europe towards the end of the eighteenth century. Michael Sadleir finds the Gothic romance as much an expression of a deep subversive impulse as was the French Revolution.

Whether or not the principles underlying the French Revolution consciously affected the outlook of the Gothic novelists and widened their conception of life is difficult to prove, yet one may say that these works are symptomatic of the confused feelings of nostalgia and terror awakened by the times, sublimated by a purely artistic impulse. It would perhaps not be wrong to state that Romanticism and Revolution are fundamentally manifestations of the same impulse. There is an unconscious indefinable relationship between the Terrors of the French Revolution and the Novel of Terror in England. The excitement and insecurity engendered by the French Revolution did quicken the nerves of literature, and the Gothic novelists were not immune from these tremors. Montague Summers shrewdly notes: "Readers, it is presumed, delighted in imaginary terrors whilst the horrors of the French Revolution were being enacted all about them."

Both in England and over the Continent dark shadows were lowering; the times were difficult, full of anxiety at the tremendous energies which were seething. Wider vistas were opening, new ideas fermenting in literature as in life. In France, unrestrained licence, rapine, and deeds of violence prevailed. It was such a period that produced the Marquis de Sade whose abnormal genius found vent in the composition of such *romans noir* whose pages of flagrant obscenity express his wild, erotic dreams. Harriet Jones, in her Preface to *The Family of Santraila* (1809), defends horrors on the grounds that they are reflections of the horror of vice and depravity. Yet while the writers were conscious of the decadence of the old order, the future seemed to offer them no hope. Bewildered and desperate, caught in the vortex of an evolving social structure, their individual frustration emerged in scenes of violence and horror.

The prominent Gothic motif of the "ruin" may be explained as being symbolic of the collapse of the feudal period; the phantom that wanders along the corridors of the haunted castle symbolizes the inexplicable fear of the return of bygone powers; the subterranean passages are the dark alleys through which the individuals stumble as they move towards the light; in the sound of thunder and in stormy settings there is the rumbling note of a distant cannon. As Michael Sadleir puts it: "A ruin expresses the triumph of chaos over order. ... Creepers and weeds, as year by year they riot over sill and paving stone, defy a broken despotism; every coping stone that crashes from a castle-battlement into the undergrowth beneath is a small victory for liberty, a snap of the fingers in the face of autocratic power." None the less the "ruin" motif was expressive of the Gothic cult of the picturesque. "I dote on ruins," says a character in Mrs. Parson's *Lucy*, "there is something sublime and awful in the sight of decayed grandeur, and large edifices tumbling to pieces." ...

Certain modern myths have grown up around Gothic romance. Dr. Kettle says the Gothic School has become "an exotic laboratory for experiments in the darkest mysteries of human and superhuman evil." It is significant that the leaders of the most modern — and not the least advertised — of modern movements, Surrealism, loudly announce their legitimate descent from the Gothic novelists, from whom, as they tell us, they derive their essential ideas, their symbolism and sentimental forms. Nevertheless, in the last chapter of *The Gothic Quest*, Montague Summers asserts that such a claim cannot be justified. "The claims put forward by the Surrealists that their new movement is influenced by and draws vital inspiration from the Gothic romance are sufficiently surprising to necessitate an inquiry into the significance and quality of this connexion — if indeed any such there be."

...The Gothic novelists produced surrealistic effects by the extensive use of grotesque contrast. Walpole had introduced the tricks of light and shade, colour and line, in his novel. Mrs. Radcliffe juxtaposed sound and silence, a kind of surrealism of atmospheric suggestion: a dead calm precedes the horrors of her tempest, sounds of retreating steps are followed by a stillness as of the grave, the music sinks low and faint as the afar off castle gates close at night and all grows still as death, a profound stillness marks the pauses of the surge breaking loud and hollow on the shore, the windows of the great hall are dark and, the torch being gone, nothing glimmers in the pitchy night save a solitary star. Even the faint, intermittent susurrus of leaves deepens the solemnity of silence. In the works of the Schauer-Romantiks, scenes of entrancing sweetness are balanced against episodes of gruesome horror; the macabre accompanies the voluptuous, as in the famous Dance of Death.

An important surrealistic technique of "telescoping" images is also employed by these authors. These novels are neither historical nor descriptive of ancient medieval manners, but essentially descriptive of the eighteenth century; and the fantastic telescoping of the two may be called a surrealistic technique.

The main doctrine of the Surrealist school is that there exists a world more real than the normal world, and this is the world of the unconscious mind. Their aim is to achieve access to the repressed contents of the unconscious, and then to mingle these elements freely with the more conscious images. In fact they, like Freudian psychologists, find a key to the perplexities of life in the material of dreams.

Dreams do constitute a definite source of the macabre and undoubtedly they inspired a number of Gothic tales. *The Castle of Otranto* was, as Walpole tells us, the result of an architectural nightmare. Mary Shelley's *Frankenstein* was likewise born out of a dream. Lafcadio Hearn, in his *Interpretations of Literature,* has asserted that all the best plots of macabre tales originate in dreams. He advises the writers of supernatural thrillers to study the phases of dream life, for nightmares provide a fertile ground for such apprenticeship. He writes: "All the great effects produced by poets and story-writers and even by religious teachers, in the treatment of the supernatural, fear or mystery have been obtained directly or indirectly from dreams."

No doubt there is a strikingly close relationship between dreams and supernatural impressions. Mystical presences usually haunt one in nocturnal hours when one arises from slumber. A guilt-laden individual starting up from sleep, imagines himself confronted with the phantoms of those he has wronged. The lover beholds the spirit of his dead beloved, for perhaps in dreams his soul has gone in quest of her. Savages, primitive men and children cannot possibly distinguish between dream and reality. Dreams are to them just actualities of experience. And it is impossible to prove that our dream life is altogether baseless and non-material.

Yet the real ancestry of Surrealism should be sought not so much in the Gothic novel as in its disintegrated form: the Gothic *fragments* of the early nineteenth century. These *fragments* are patchwork exercises in evoking atmosphere by disconnected episodes of terror. Neither accounting for their mysterious horrors nor attempting the construction of a thrilling plot sequence, these evoke precisely the same feelings through the medium of words as do the paintings of Picasso, Marc Chagall, Chirico, Klee or Max Ernst.

There have been sporadic attempts to give a Freudian interpretation to Gothic motif and machinery. The present writer has not fully attempted this application, and therefore cannot judge of its validity; nevertheless it is necessary and interesting to note how the forces of nature as painted by the Gothic novelists are capable of being given a Freudian twist. The turbulent settings in which the tempter appears in Gothic novels, combine "in the highest degree the struggle between the instinct of death on the one hand, which, as Freud has shown, is also an instinct of preservation, and, on the other, Eros, who exacts after each human hecatomb the glorious restoration of life." The thunder itself by its violence and loudness of pitch giving a profound physical stimulus to the ear, and "lightning," often known as a "thunderbolt" which has a sudden and supremely devastating power, have been associated with the most terrifying things possible: as Mr. Hugh Sykes Davies puts it, "the magnified image of the enraged father." An angered father threatening punishment is the symbol of all power and terror for a child; for an adult "thunder" no longer evokes the image of an angered father, but transforms itself into that of an angry God. The terror of death and the grave are closely allied to the theological representation of the divinity as the God of Wrath. Even the spiral staircase has been called symbolic of neurotic sensibility.

Melancholy, gloom, rape, and spiritual sufferings have earned for these works their Continental title of *"Les romans noir."* They are in English fiction the first manifestation of what Mario Praz has termed "The Romantic Agony" of literature, and what Dr. Kettle refers to as "that often terrible exploration of the darker sides of the human mind and experience, which later finds expression in such a novel as *Wuthering Heights."*

The Idea of the Numinous
in Gothic Literature

by S. L. Varnado

One of the engaging aspects of modern literary criticism has been the enthusiastic acceptance of aid from nonliterary disciplines. Psychoanalysis, anthropology, sociology, and semantics have undoubtedly enriched our understanding and influenced our critical response to literature[1] One suspects, however, that such methodologies are best applied to works which are more or less subjective in nature. The Gothic tradition in British and American literature, for instance, offers itself as a prime candidate. Critical appraisal of Gothic literature has sometimes been marked by an ambiguity, as though critics found difficulty in coming to terms with the material. In a well-known pronouncement on Edgar Allan Poe, T. S. Eliot has stated a common attitude toward Gothic fiction: "The forms which his lively curiosity takes are those in which a preadolescent mentality delights: wonders of nature and of mechanics and of the supernatural, cryptograms, and cyphers, puzzles and labyrinths, mechanical chess-players, and wild flights of speculation. ... There is just that lacking which gives dignity to the mature man: a consistent view of life. ..."[2] The Gothic elements in Poe's writings seem to be at

[1]See Stanley Edgar Hymen, *The Armed Vision, A Study in the Methods of Modern Literary Criticism* (New York: Vintage Books, 1948), p. 3.

[2]"From Poe to Valéry," *Hudson Review*, 2 (1949), 335.

the root of Eliot's rejection. On the other hand, a writer whom Eliot admires, Charles Baudelaire, takes a different view toward this same sort of material. For Baudelaire, "what will always make him [Poe] worthy of praise is his preoccupation with all the truly important subjects and those which are *alone* worthy of the attention of a spiritual man: probabilities, mental illnesses, scientific hypotheses, hopes and considerations about a future life, analysis of the eccentrics and pariahs of this world. ..."[3]

Such an antinomy raises, in fact, the central question about the Gothic spirit as it is reflected in the work of early novelists such as Horace Walpole, Ann Radcliffe, and Mary Shelley, as well as later writers like Charlotte Brontë, Edgar Allan Poe, Algernon Blackwood, and Franz Kafka. What, precisely, is the common denominator of a literary tradition that includes such a diverse company, and that has attracted, at least for a time, such dissimilar minds as those of Charles Dickens, Henry James, Joseph Conrad, and William Faulkner? The answer, as suggested, demands in part an analysis by way of nonliterary disciplines, since it is evident that the literary powers of such writers are not in question.

The particular nonliterary discipline that I propose for analyzing the Gothic tradition consists of the impressive body of work left by the late German theologian and philosopher Rudolf Otto (1869-1937). In his major work, *The Idea of the Holy* (1917), Otto attempted to analyze religious experience by means of what he termed the numinous. His central concern in the book is indicated by its subtitle: "The nonrational factor in the idea of the divine and its relation to the rational." The numinous, the word he coined to represent this nonrational factor, is man's underlying sense of supernatural fear, wonder, and delight when he is confronted by the divine. Although the several elements in numinous feeling may be analyzed, the numinous is essentially nonrational—that is, not able to be fully understood conceptually. It is a "feeling" but a feeling that has innate connections with the intellect. The numinous, which in its more primitive forms gives rise to the belief in ghosts and other supernatural fantasies, is still present in purified form in the higher manifestations of religion. This experience, with its associated forms and connec-

---

[3]*Baudelaire on Poe*. trans. and ed. Lois and Francis E. Hyslop, Jr. (State College, Pa.: Bald Eagle Press, 1952), p. 151.

tions, its dichotomies between "sacred and profane," between "natural and supernatural," "rational and non-rational," and its often fragile but sometimes strong relations to the human sense of the "holy" is, I believe, the essential goal of the Gothic writer, and so far as it is achieved, his central distinction.

Otto's terminology and some of his ideas have appeared in works of literary criticism. There is, for instance, a very sound discussion of Otto's works in Maud Bodkin's *Archetypal Patterns in Poetry*. Both G. Wilson Knight and Walter Kaufman have used Otto's terminology in exploring certain aspects of Shakespeare.[4] But even if the legitimacy of the numinous as a literary concept is granted, the question of relating it to the Gothic tale may appear doubtful. In what sense, it will be asked, does the preternatural element in Gothic fiction enter into the psychology of religious experience? Indeed, it will appear almost paradoxical to attempt to relate the two, since the more evident varieties of religious experience—prayer, contemplation, and mysticism— whether orthodox or otherwise, seem remote from the Gothic experience of Romantic literature.

It is in answer to this problem that the insights of Rudolf Otto are applicable. For Otto was certain that the area of religious experience which he termed the numinous is, in its early stages, closely associated with the preternatural; and that while some religions in their more advanced stages outgrow this association, they still retain vestiges of it. In fact, Otto was convinced that the preternatural as a condition of human consciousness is intimately connected with the whole phenomenon of religion.

Otto begins *The Idea of the Holy* by distinguishing conceptual from nonconceptual statements about religion. Theistic religion, he believes, characterizes God by various conceptual statements about his nature, for example, his spirituality, power, and unity. Such conceptual statements Otto terms rational, and he makes it clear that they are of first importance in religious discussion. On the other hand, the nature of God is such that these rational attributes do not fully comprehend Him. "For so far are these

[4]See Maud Bodkin, *Archetypal Patterns in Poetry* (London: Oxford Univ. Press, 1934), pp. 223, 241; Walter Kaufman, *From Shakespeare to Existentialism* (Boston: Beacon Press, 1949), p. 37; G. Wilson Knight, *The Crown of Life* (London: Methuen, 1947), p. 128.

'rational' attributes from exhausting the idea of deity, that they in fact imply a non-rational or suprarational Subject of which they are predicates." This nonrational element, however, must be apprehended in some way "else absolutely speaking nothing could be asserted of it."[5]

To characterize this nonrational element or "unnamed Something" as he calls it, Otto coins the word *numinous,* from the Latin *numen* (a god or power). "I shall speak, then, of a unique 'numinous' category of value and of a definitely 'numinous' state of mind, which is always found wherever the category is applied. This mental state is perfectly *sui generis* and irreducible to any other; and therefore, like every absolutely primary and elementary datum, while it admits of being discussed, it cannot be strictly defined" (p. 7). But if the numinous cannot be defined it can, nevertheless, be suggested. "We must once again endeavour, by adducing feelings akin to them for the purpose of analogy or contrast and by the use of metaphor and symbolic expressions, to make the states of mind we are investigating ring out, as it were, of themselves" (p. 12).

In attempting to suggest these numinous states of mind, Otto uses as an ideogram the Latin phrase *mysterium tremendum.* "Conceptually *mysterium* is merely that which is hidden and esoteric, that which is beyond conception or understanding, extraordinary and unfamiliar. The term does not define the object more positively in its qualitative character. But though what is enunciated in the word is negative, what is meant is something absolutely and intensely positive. This pure positive we can experience in feelings, feelings which our discussion can help make clear to us, in so far as it arouses them actually in our hearts" (p. 13).

A number of distinct "notes" or feeling-states enter into Otto's analysis of the phrase *mysterium tremendum. Tremor,* for example, is the Latin word for the familiar experience of the natural emotion of fear. However, Otto uses it to suggest "a quite specific kind of emotional response, wholly distinct from that of being afraid. ... There are in some languages special expressions which denote, either exclusively or in the first instance, this 'fear' that is

[5]Rudolf Otto, *The Idea of the Holy,* trans. John W. Harvey (New York: Oxford Univ. Press, 1958), p. 2.

more than fear proper. The Hebrew *Hiqdīsh* (hallow) is an example. To 'keep a thing holy in the heart' means to mark it off by a feeling of peculiar dread, not to be mistaken for any ordinary dread, that is, to appraise it by the category of the numinous" (p. 13).

The subtle, but distinct, qualitative difference between this feeling and ordinary human fear is suggested by an analysis of the physical reactions that accompany these states.

> We say: "my blood ran icy cold," and "my flesh crept." The "cold blood" feeling may be a symptom of ordinary, natural fear, but there is something non-natural or supernatural about the symptoms of "creeping flesh." And any one who is capable of more precise introspection must recognize that the distinction between such a "dread" and natural fear is not simply one of degree and intensity. The awe or "dread" *may* indeed be so overwhelmingly great that it seems to penetrate to the very marrow, making the man's hair bristle and his limbs quake. But it may also steal upon him almost unobserved as the gentlest of agitations, a mere fleeting shadow passing across his mood. It has therefore nothing to do with intensity, and no natural fear passes over into it merely by being intensified. (p. 16)

The accuracy of Otto's description is attested to by a number of passages from Gothic fiction. Cold blood and creeping flesh are, in fact, staples of Gothic literature, but it is the exceptional reader who has distinguished between "ordinary human fear" and the numinous emotions. A passage from Algernon Blackwood's short story "The Willows" suggests some remarkable parallels with what Otto has to say about numinous awe. In this tale, the narrator and a companion proceed by canoe into the upper reaches of the Danube where, amidst the loneliness of the primitive forest and a rising windstorm, they come upon a remote island entirely covered by small willow trees. They make camp, and as night falls the narrator attempts to analyze the alien emotions aroused in him by the island.

> Great revelations of nature, of course, never fail to impress in one way or another, and I was no stranger to moods of the kind. Mountains overawe and oceans terrify, while the mystery of great forests exercises a spell peculiarly its own. But all these, at one point or

another, somewhere link on intimately with human life and human experience. They stir comprehensible, even if alarming, emotions. They tend on the whole to exalt.

With this multitude of willows, however, it was something far different, I felt. Some essence emanated from them that besieged the heart. A sense of awe awakened, true, but of awe touched somewhere by a vague terror. Their serried ranks, growing everywhere darker about me as the shadows deepened, moving furiously yet softly in the wind, woke in me the curious and unwelcome suggestion that we had trespassed here upon the borders of an alien world, a world where we were intruders, a world where we were not wanted or invited to remain—where we ran grave risks perhaps![6]

This sense of the "uncanny" or "awesome" does not, however, exhaust the feeling states aroused by the ideogram *tremendum*. Otto perceives another element in it, namely the sense of "might," "power," "absolute overpoweringness," to which he gives the name of *majestas*.

This second element of majesty may continue to be vividly preserved, where the first, that of unapproachability, recedes and dies away, as may be seen for example in mysticism. It is especially in relation to this element of majesty or absolute overpoweringness that the creature-consciousness, of which we have already spoken, comes upon the scene, as a sort of shadow or subjective reflection of it. Thus, in contrast to the "overpowering" of which we are conscious, as an object over against the self, there is the feeling of one's own submergence, of being but "dust and ashes" and nothingness. And this forms the numinous raw material for the feeling of religious humility. (p. 20)

Otto's representation of *majestas* must not be confused with the sense of "natural" majesty, although such awareness may be its starting point. This fugitive feeling-state is hard to depict in a single passage of literature. It generally finds its context in a cumulative series of narrations, as in the final chapters of *Moby Dick*. The emotion does seem well focussed, however, in the description of the first sight of the numinous and nearly supernal whale.

[6]Algernon Blackwood, *Tales of Terror and the Unknown* (New York: E. P. Dutton & Co., 1965), pp. 20-21.

A gentle joyousness—a mighty mildness of repose in swiftness, invested the gliding whale. Not the white bull Jupiter swimming away with ravished Europa clinging to his graceful horns; his lovely, leering eyes sideways intent upon the maid; with smooth bewitching fleetness, rippling straight for the nuptial bower in Crete; not Jove, not that great majesty Supreme! did surpass the glorified White Whale as he so divinely swam.

On each soft side—coincident with the parted swell, that but once leaving him, then flowed so wide away—on each bright side, the whale shed off encitings. No wonder there had been some among the hunters who namelessly transported and allured by all this serenity, had ventured to assail it; but had fatally found that quietude but the vesture of tornadoes. Yet calm, enticing calm, oh, whale! thou glidest on, to all who for the first time eye thee, no matter how many in that same way thou may'st have bejuggled and destroyed before.[7]

A final element suggested by the ideogram *tremendum* is termed by Otto the "urgency" or "energy" of the numinous object. This element is sometimes projected symbolically as the "wrath of God," and in qualities of vitality, passion, emotional temper, will-force, movement, excitement, activity, and impetus. Such a feeling, Otto tells us, makes its appearance in mysticism, especially "voluntaristic" mysticism and "the mysticism of love." It appears in Fichte's speculations on the Absolute as the gigantic, never-resting, active world-stress, and in Schopenhauer's daemonic "Will." In Goethe, too, the same note is sounded in his strange description of the "daemonic."[8] The quality isolated here is prominent in Gothic fiction. Some of it enters into the characterization of Mr. Rochester in *Jane Eyre,* and of the monster in Mary Shelley's *Frankenstein.* It appears in rather melodramatic form in the final chapter of *The Monk* when the fiend carries Ambrosio out of the dungeon and across the mountain peaks. And it certainly contributes to the character of Captain Ahab, the "grand ungodly god-like man" of *Moby Dick.*

Thus Otto distinguishes three distinct, but related, moments suggested by the ideogram *tremendum:* awfulness, majesty, and

---

[7]Herman Melville, *Moby Dick,* ed. Charles Feidelson, Jr. (Indianapolis: The Bobbs-Merrill Company, Inc., 1964), p. 690.

[8]As described by Otto, pp. 23-24.

energy. He now proceeds to an analysis of the substantive *myster-ium,* which stands as the form of the numinous experience. The mental reaction to this "moment" in the numinous consciousness is best described analogically by the word "stupor." "Stupor is plainly a different thing from *tremor;* it signifies blank wonder, an astonishment that strikes us dumb, amazement absolute." Its objective concomitant, the *mysterium,* suggests that which is "wholly other" *(anyad, alienum)* or in other words "that which is quite beyond the sphere of the usual, the intelligible, and the familiar, which therefore falls quite outside the limits of the 'canny' and is contrasted with it, filling the mind with blank wonder and astonishment" (p. 26).

To suggest this sense of the "wholly other" Otto undertakes an analysis of the fear of ghosts—a subject obviously quite germane to the Gothic.

> The ghost's real attraction...consists in this, that of itself and in an uncommon degree it entices the imagination, awakening strong interest and curiosity; it is the weird thing itself that allures the fancy. But it does this, not because it is "something long and white" (as someone once defined a ghost) nor yet through any of the positive conceptual attributes which fancies about ghosts have invented, but because it is a thing that "doesn't really exist at all," the "wholly other," something which has no place in our scheme of reality but belongs to an absolutely different one and which at the same time arouses an irrepressible interest in the mind. (pp. 28-29).

The accuracy of Rudolf Otto's analysis of such ghostly matters is attested to by a great deal of literature of the supernatural, but no better paradigm is available than Henry James' classic ghost story "The Jolly Corner." The description of Spencer Brydon's encounter with his horrific doppelgänger clearly depicts both the "wholly other" character of the spirit as well as the sense of blank wonder and stupor.

> The hands, as he looked, began to move, to open; then, as if deciding in a flash, dropped from the face and left it uncovered and presented. Horror, with the sight, had leaped into Brydon's throat, gasping there in a sound he couldn't utter; for the bared identity was too hideous as *his,* and his glare was the passion of his protest. The face, *that* face, Spencer Brydon's?—he searched it still, but looking away from it in dismay and denial, falling straight from his

height of sublimity. It was unknown, inconceivable, awful, disconnected from any possibility—! He had been "sold," he inwardly
moaned, stalking such game as this: the presence before him was
a presence, the horror within him a horror, but the waste of his
nights had been only grotesque and the success of his adventure an
irony. Such an identity fitted his at *no* point, made its alternative
monstrous. A thousand times yes, as it came upon him nearer now
—the face was the face of a stranger. It came upon him nearer now,
quite as one of those expanding fantastic images projected by the
magic lantern of childhood; for the stranger, whoever he might be,
evil, odious, blatant, vulgar, had advanced as for aggression, and
he knew himself give ground, ... he felt the whole vision turn to
darkness and his very feet give way. His head went round; he was
going; he had gone.[9]

In this passage, as in the entire story, the *mysterium* is transformed into and partakes of James' private universe, with all its
exquisite values and peculiar defects. No writer could be further,
in some ways, from the "average Gothic," and yet the numinous
qualities provide a link. The apparition is "unknown, inconceivable, awful, disconnected from any possibility—!" which one takes
to be a Jamesian rendition of the "wholly other." In fact, as
James himself attests in several of his prefaces, the supernatural
tale fascinated him.

It is the sense of fascination that forms the final strand in Otto's
analysis of numinous feeling. Having analyzed what might be
termed the daunting aspect of the numinous *(mysterium tremendum)*, Otto discusses another element that stands at the
opposite pole. This element Otto designates by the term *fascinans,*
a kind of fascination, attraction, or allurement in the numinous.
This *fascinans* is "a bliss which embraces all those blessings that
are indicated or suggested in a positive fashion by any 'doctrine
of salvation,' and it quickens all of them through and through; but
these do not exhaust it. Rather by its all pervading, penetrating
glow it makes of these very blessings more than the intellect can
conceive in them or affirm of them" (pp. 33-34).

Thus, Otto groups in what he calls a "harmony of contrasts" the
various moments in the numinous experience; and these he indi-

---

[9]Henry James, *Ghostly Tales of Henry James,* ed. Leon Edel (New York: Gros-
set & Dunlap, 1963), pp. 427-28.

cates by the phrase (or ideogram as he terms it) *mysterium tremendum et fascinosum.*

> These two qualities, the daunting and the fascinating, now combine in a strange harmony of contrasts, and the resultant dual character of the numinous consciousness, to which the entire religious development bears witness, at any rate from the level of the "daemonic dread" onwards, is at once the strangest and the most noteworthy phenomenon in the whole history of religion. The daemonic-divine object may appear to the mind an object of horror and dread, but at the same time it is no less something that allures with a potent charm, and the creature who trembles before it, utterly cowed and cast down, has always at the same time the impulse to turn to it, nay even to make it somehow his own. The "mystery" is for him not merely something to be wondered at but something that entrances him; and beside that in it which bewilders and confounds, he feels a something that captivates and transports him with a strange ravishment, rising often enough to the pitch of intoxication: it is the Dionysiac-element in the numen. (p. 31)

The peculiar "harmony of contrasts" is a prominent feature in the work of Edgar Allan Poe, who certainly had an intuitive grasp of the numinous consciousness as Otto expounds it, and explains, to some degree, Poe's puzzling ideas concerning "perversity" ("The Imp of the Perverse"), ideas which interested Baudelaire. But on a higher plane this daunting-attracting quality of the numinous infuses most of Poe's tales and poems. A striking example is his tale "A Descent Into the Maelstrom." As the protagonist finds himself drawn into the immense and terrifying depths of the maelstrom, the reflections vary from awe and terror before this nearly preternatural manifestation to a strange sense of fascination.

> It may look like boasting—but what I tell you is truth—I began to reflect how magnificent a thing it was to die in such a manner, and how foolish it was in me to think of so paltry a consideration as my own individual life, in view of so wonderful a manifestation of God's power. I do believe that I blushed with shame when this idea crossed my mind. After a little while I became possessed with the keenest curiosity about the whirl itself. I positively felt a *wish* to explore its depths, even at the sacrifice I was going to make; and

my principal grief was that I should never be able to tell my old companions on shore about the mysteries I should see.[10]

Throughout his book, Otto continually emphasizes that the numinous is not identical with the fully developed sense of the Holy. The concept of Holiness must of necessity include theological and moral elements. The numinous may thus be seen as bearing intrinsic relationship with and even providing a definition for a number of works, both literary and artistic, which might not generally be termed religious. For what else is one to say of the castles and mountain crags of Mrs. Radcliffe's novels, the glaciers, ice-floes, and desolate Scottish islands of *Frankenstein,* or the spectral sea-scapes of *The Narrative of Arthur Gordon Pym* but that they summon up many of the moods and tones that Otto has analyzed? Thus, by making use of Otto's insights, one is able to sense a new and more profound note in some very good literature of this kind that has sometimes been looked at with bewilderment it not downright condescension by certain critics.

Another fruitful link between the numinous and the Gothic tradition is to be found in Otto's remarks about preternatural events and magic. Preternaturalism has, of course, been a source of annoyance to some critics of the Gothic; and it does, indeed, require a strong palate to accept all the bleeding portraits, animated skeletons, lycanthropes, rattling chains, and vampires that infest Gothic literature, especially the older novels. But the artistic incorporation of the preternatural into literature should not, in itself, form a barrier to critical appreciation. It is on this point that Otto supplies a strong apologetic. "Now the magical," he says, "is nothing but a suppressed and dimmed form of the numinous, a crude form of it which great art purifies and ennobles." He adds, "To us of the West the Gothic appears as the most numinous of all types of art. This is due in the first place to its sublimity; but Worringer in his *Problem der Ghotik* has done a real service in showing that the peculiar impressiveness of Gothic does not consist in its sublimity alone, but draws upon a strain inherited from primitive magic, of which he tries to show the historical derivation" (pp. 67-68).

[10]Edgar Allan Poe, *The Complete Works of Edgar Allan Poe,* ed. James A. Harrison (New York: Thomas Y. Crowell & Co., 1902), II, 240.

The magical or preternatural event, then, if introduced artistically may serve to reinforce the numinous quality of the work. Nathaniel Hawthorne, who was sparing in his use of the preternatural, seems to achieve the proper effect in a passage from *The Marble Faun.* Donatello, Miriam, and Kenyon approach the open bier of a dead monk who lies in the Church of the Capuchins in Rome.

> And now occurred a circumstance that would seem too fantastic to be told, if it had not actually happened, precisely as we set it down. As the three friends stood by the bier, they saw that a little stream of blood had begun to ooze from the dead monk's nostrils; it crept slowly towards the thicket of his beard, where, in the course of a moment or two, it hid itself.
>
> "How strange!" ejaculated Kenyon. "The monk died of apoplexy, I suppose, or by some sudden accident, and the blood has not yet congealed."
>
> "Do you consider that a sufficient explanation?" asked Miriam, with a smile from which the sculptor involuntarily turned away his eyes. "Does it satisfy you?"
>
> "And why not?" he inquired.
>
> "Of course, you know the old superstition about this phenomenon of blood flowing from a dead body," she rejoined. "How can we tell but that the murderer of this monk (or, possibly, it may be only that privileged murderer, his physician) may have just entered the church?"[11]

The Idea of the Holy contains chapters, of special interest to the literary critic, on the means of arousing the numinous consciousness by artistic works. "Of directer methods our Western art has only two," Otto says, "and they are in a noteworthy way negative, viz. *darkness* and *silence.*" His discussion of the artistic use of darkness conjures up many images of the "haunted castle" theme so dear to the tale of terror: "The semi-darkness that glimmers in vaulted halls, or beneath the branches of a lofty forest glade, strangely quickened and stirred by the mysterious play of half-lights, has always spoken eloquently to the soul, and the builders of temples, mosques and churches have made full use of it" (p. 68). Silence is "what corresponds to this in the language of

[11]Nathaniel Hawthorne, *The Writings of Nathaniel Hawthorne* (Boston: Houghton Mifflin and Company, 1903), IX, 263.

musical sounds. ...It is a spontaneous reaction to the feeling of the actual *numen praesens"* (pp. 68-69). Both of these "artistic means" are native to Western art; but Oriental art makes continual use of a third, namely, empty distance and emptiness. "Empty distance, remote vacancy, is, as it were, the sublime in the horizontal. The wide-stretching desert, the boundless uniformity of the steppe, have a real sublimity, and even in us Westerners they set vibrating chords of the numinous along with the note of the sublime, according to the principle of the association of feelings" (p. 69).

Perhaps Otto is right in concluding that most Western art has generally failed to make consistent use of emptiness, but the Gothic literary tradition has, indeed, effectively utilized this method as a means to register a sense of the numinous. The vacant loneliness associated with sea, desert, mountain prospects, or the night sky is a constant theme. This characteristic is especially true of Coleridge's *Ancient Mariner* ("Alone, alone, all, all alone/ Alone on a wide wide sea!") and Poe's *Narrative of Arthur Gordon Pym,* as well as of several of Joseph Conrad's novels in which brooding descriptions of the sea stimulate the numinous sense of emptiness and silence. In *Victory,* for instance, a work which contains certain strong numinous elements, the lonely protagonist Heyst is a man who feels this numinous call of the sea.

> Like most dreamers, to whom it is given sometimes to hear the music of the spheres, Heyst, the wanderer of the Archipelago, had a taste for silence which he had been able to gratify for years. The islands are very quiet. One sees them lying about, clothed in their dark garments of leaves, in a great hush of silver and azure, where the sea without murmurs meets the sky in a ring of magic stillness. A sort of smiling somnolence broods over them; the very voices of their people are soft and subdued, as if afraid to break some protecting spell.[12]

Thus, it seems clear that Otto's work provides many insights into the spirit of Gothic literature. The mountain gloom, lonely castles, phantom ships, violent storms, and the vastness of sea and polar regions correspond closely with Otto's description of the numinous. Likewise, the preternatural machinery of Gothicism,

---

[12]Joseph Conrad, *Victory* (New York: The Modern Library, 1921), p. 64.

whether magical lore, apparitions, ghouls, vampires, or reven-
ants, finds its explanation not in an over-ripe fantasy, but in an
effort to instill a sense of the numinous.

We have seen several ways in which the numinous plays a part
both in background and event in the Gothic tale. But the numinous is not confined to ontological reality; Otto contends that it
also has an axiological character. This is to say, the numinous
exists as a category of value within its own right; and as a consequence it can be used in analyzing character and moral value.

According to Otto, the numinous experience in itself is not an
ethical manifestation and may exist without any relation to
morality, as for instance in the case of certain primitive religions.
When the numinous is commingled with moral and rational elements it becomes something different—namely *The Holy*. On the
other hand, the numinous in its pure form, and without moral
connotations, is still permeated by certain axiological elements.
The numinous "object" produces in the percipient a sense of
"creature feelings"; in fact, this result is one of the essential ways
in which it impinges upon the individual consciousness. Out of
such a feeling grows the sense of numinous value and of numinous disvalue. In opposition to this sense of "disvalue" or the
profane stands the sacred. "This sanctus is not merely 'perfect' or
'beautiful' or 'sublime' or 'good,' though being like these concepts
also a value, objective and ultimate, it has a definite, perceptible
analogy with them. It is the positive numinous value or worth,
and to it corresponds on the side of the creature a numinous disvalue or 'unworth' " (Otto, p. 51).

The sense of numinous value, the sacred, is recognized as standing outside the sphere of morality as such. "In every highly-
developed religion the appreciation of moral obligation and duty,
ranking as a claim of the deity upon man, has been developed
side by side with the religious feeling itself. Nonetheless, a profoundly humble and heartfelt recognition of 'the holy' may occur
in particular experiences without being always definitely charged
or infused with the sense of moral demands. The 'holy' will then
be recognized as that which commands our respect, as that whose
real value is to be acknowledged inwardly" (p. 51). Likewise, the
opposite pole, the numinous "disvalue" or sense of the profane, is
not intrinsically a moral category. "Mere 'unlawfulness' only
becomes 'sin,' 'impiety,' 'sacrilege,' when the character of *numin-*

ous unworthiness or disvalue goes on to be transferred to and centered in moral delinquency" (p. 52).

Otto's explanation of numinous value and disvalue, if viewed as a phenomenological description, applies with equal force to many Gothic works which might otherwise appear to be morally neutral and therefore, at best, mere entertainment. There are, it is true, certain patent moral lessons attached to Mary Shelley's *Frankenstein*, but the categories of the sacred and profane, if applied to the hero's unholy experiments, add a new dimension to the story.

To explore this interpretation briefly, we must remember that the story projects a feeling of horror and evil that is disproportionate to the moral framework out of which Mary Shelley worked. The crimes of the monster and the ultimate ruin of his creator Frankenstein are the results of an experiment begun, perhaps, in good conscience. Mary Shelley suggests, in fact, that some of the evil nature of the monster is the result of economic and moral dislocations in society. Then, too, as a rationalist and liberal who followed the views of her father, she would have rejected a belief in the innate evil of man. What then is responsible for the brooding sense of profanity and unhallowed occupation that characterizes the inception of the monster?

> Who shall conceive the horrors of my secret toil, as I dabbled among the unhallowed damps of the grave, or tortured the living animal to animate the lifeless clay? My limbs now tremble and my eyes swim with the remembrance; but then a resistless, and almost frantic, impulse urged me forward; I seemed to have lost all soul or sensation but for this one pursuit. ...I collected bones from charnel-houses, and disturbed, with profane fingers, the tremendous secrets of the human frame. In a solitary chamber, or rather cell, at the top of the house, and separated from all the other apartments by a gallery and staircase, I kept my workshop of filthy creation: my eye-balls were starting from their sockets in attending to the details of my employment.[13]

There is really no "rational" explanation for such feelings, given the moral views of Frankenstein. He feels, rather, the sense of numinous "disvalue" attendant upon his profane experiments, a feeling that Mary Shelley shared despite her liberal and utopian

---

[13]Mary W. Shelley, *Frankenstein* (London: Everyman's Library, 1963), p. 48.

sentiments to the contrary. The famous description of the anima-
tion of the monster heightens this sense of profanity.

> It was already one in the morning; the rain pattered dismally
> against the panes, and my candle was nearly burnt out, when, by
> the glimmer of the half-extinguished light, I saw the dull yellow
> eye of the creature open; it breathed hard, and a convulsive motion
> agitated its limbs.
>
> How can I describe my emotions at this catastrophe, or how
> delineate the wretch whom with such infinite pains and care I had
> endeavoured to form? His limbs were in proportion, and I had
> selected his features as beautiful. Beautiful—Great God! His yellow
> skin scarcely covered the work of muscles and arteries beneath, his
> hair was of a lustrous black, and flowing; his teeth of a pearly
> whiteness; but these luxuriances only formed a more horrid con-
> trast with his watery eyes, that seemed almost of the same colour as
> the dun white sockets in which they were set, his shrivelled com-
> plexion and straight black lips. (p. 51)

The question of Frankenstein's guilt in tampering with the well-
springs of life is not treated directly. The consequent crimes and
atrocities perpetrated by the monster are the results of "man's
inhumanity to man," the evils of society and, to a certain extent,
mere chance. Even at the last, Fankenstein absolves himself of
direct guilt: "During these last days I have been occupied in
examining my past conduct; nor do I find it blameable. In a fit
of enthusiastic madness I created a rational creature, and was
bound towards him, to assure, as far as was in my power, his
happiness and well-being. This was my duty; but there was another still paramount to that. My duties towards the beings of my
own species had greater claims to my attention, because they
included a greater proportion of happiness or misery" (p. 235).
Thus, on the merely rational level, *Frankenstein* expounds some
rather patent moral truths which are perhaps most interesting
from a historical standpoint. But in a deeper sense, the book
portrays the mysterious sense of "profanity" and numinous disvalue which, according to Otto, is part of man's spiritual life.

It is upon such a system of thought, profound and original, that
a new survey of Gothic literature may be conducted. Otto's
description of the numinous, self-authenticating and convincing,
suggests a new dimension to the literature of the preternatural.

The Beating of Black Wings: Supernatural Horror in Literature and the Fiction of Edgar Allan Poe

by H. P. Lovecraft

The oldest and strongest emotion of mankind is fear, and the oldest and strongest kind of fear is fear of the unknown. These facts few psychologists will dispute, and their admitted truth must establish for all time the genuineness and dignity of the weirdly horrible tales as a literary form. Against it are discharged all the shafts of a materialistic sophistication which clings to frequently felt emotions and external events, and of a naively inspired idealism which deprecates the aesthetic motive and calls for a didactic literature to "uplift" the reader toward a suitable degree of smirking optimism. But in spite of all this opposition the weird tale has survived, developed, and attained remarkable heights of perfection; founded as it is on a profound and elementary principle whose appeal, if not always universal, must necessarily be poignant and permanent to minds of the requisite sensitiveness.

The appeal of the spectrally macabre is generally narrow because it demands from the reader a certain degree of imagination and a capacity for detachment from everyday life. Relatively few are free enough from the spell of the daily routine to respond to rappings from outside, and tales of ordinary feelings and events, or of common sentimental distortions of such feelings and events, will always take first place in the taste of the majority; rightly, perhaps, since of course these ordinary matters make up the greater part of human experience. But the sensitive are always with us, and sometimes a curious streak of fancy invades an obscure corner of the very hardest head; so that no amount of rationalisation, reform, or Freudian analysis can quite annul the thrill of the chimney-corner whisper or the lonely wood. There is here involved psychological pattern or tradition as real and as deeply grounded in mental experience as any other pattern or tradition of mankind; coeval with the religious feeling and closely related to many aspects of it, and too much a part of our innermost biological heritage to lose keen potency over a very important, though not numerically great, minority of our species.

Man's first instincts and emotions formed his response to the environment in which he found himself. Definite feelings based on pleasure and pain grew up around the phenomena whose causes and effects he understood, whilst around those which he did not understand — and the universe teemed with them in the early days — were naturally woven such personifications, marvelous interpretations, and sensations of awe and fear as would be hit upon by a race having few and simple ideas and limited experience. The unknown, being likewise the unpredictable, became for our primitive forefathers a terrible and omnipotent source of boons and calamities visited upon mankind for cryptic and wholly extraterrestrial reasons, and thus clearly belonging to spheres of existence whereof we know nothing and wherein we have no part. The phenomenon of dreaming likewise helped to build up the notion of an unreal or spiritual world; and in general, all the conditions of savage dawn-life so strongly conducted toward a feeling of the supernatural, that we need not wonder at the thoroughness with which man's very hereditary essence has become saturated with religion and superstition. That saturation must, as a matter of plain scientific fact, be regarded as virtually permanent so far as the subconscious mind and inner instincts are concerned; for though the area of the unknown has been steadily contracting for thousands of years, an infinite reservoir of mystery still engulfs most of the outer cosmos, whilst a vast residuum of powerful inherited associations clings round all the objects and processes that were once mysterious, however well they may now be explained. And more than this, there is an actual physiological fixation of the old instincts in our nervous tissue, which would make them obscurely operative even were the conscious mind to be purged of all sources of wonder.

Because we remember pain and the menace of death more vividly than pleasure, and because our feelings toward the beneficent aspects of the unknown have from the first been captured and formalised by conventional religious rituals, it has fallen to the lot of the darker and more maleficent side of cosmic mystery to figure chiefly in our popular supernatural folklore. This tendency, too, is naturally enhanced by the fact that uncertainty and danger are always closely allied; thus making any kind of an unknown world a world of peril and evil possibilities. When to this sense of fear and evil the inevitable fascination of wonder and curiosity is superadded, there is born a composite body of keen emotion and imaginative provocation whose vitality must of necessity endure as long as the human race itself. Children will always be afraid of the dark, and men with minds sensitive to hereditary impulse will always tremble at the thought of the hidden and fathomless worlds of strange life which may pulsate in the gulfs beyond the stars, or press hideously upon our own globe in unholy dimensions which only the dead and the moonstruck can glimpse.

With this foundation, no one need wonder at the existence of a literature of cosmic fear. It has always existed, and always will exist; and no better evidence of its tenacious vigour can be cited than the impulse which now and then drives writers of totally opposite leanings to try their hands at it in isolated tales, as if to discharge from their minds certain phantasmal shapes which would otherwise haunt them. Thus Dickens wrote several eerie narratives; Browning, the hideous poem *Childe Roland;* Henry James, *The Turn of the Screw;* Dr. Holmes, the subtle novel *Elsie Venner;* F. Marion Crawford, *The Upper Berth* and a number of other examples; Mrs. Charlotte Perkins Gilman, social worker, *The Yellow Wall Paper;* whilst the humorist, W. W. Jacobs, produced that able melodramatic bit called *The Monkey's Paw.*

This type of fear-literature must not be confounded with a type

externally similar but psychologically widely different; the literature of mere physical fear and the mundanely gruesome. Such
writing, to be sure, has its place, as has the conventional or even
whimsical or humorous ghost story where formalism or the
author's knowing wink removes the true sense of the morbidly
unnatural; but these things are not the literature of cosmic fear
in its purest sense. The true weird tale has something more than
secret murder, bloody bones, or a sheeted form clanking chains
according to rule. A certain atmosphere of breathless and unexplainable dread of outer, unknown forces must be present; and
there must be a hint, expressed with a seriousness and portentous-
ness becoming its subject, of that most terrible conception of the
human brain—a malign and particular suspension or defeat of
those fixed laws of Nature which are our only safeguard against
the assaults of chaos and the daemons of unplumbed space.

Naturally we cannot expect all weird tales to conform absolutely to any theoretical model. Creative minds are uneven, and the
best of fabrics have their dull spots. Moreover, much of the
choicest weird work is unconscious; appearing in memorable
fragments scattered through material whose massed effect may be
of a very different cast. Atmosphere is the all-important thing, for
the final criterion of authenticity is not the dovetailing of a plot
but the creation of a given sensation. We may say, as a general
thing, that a weird story whose intent is to teach or produce a
social effect, or one in which the horrors are finally explained
away by natural means, is not a genuine tale of cosmic fear; but
it remains a fact that such narratives often possess, in isolated
sections, atmospheric touches which fulfill every condition of
true supernatural horror-literature. Therefore we must judge a
weird tale not by the author's intent, or by the mere mechanics of
the plot; but by the emotional level which it attains at its least
mundane point. If the proper sensations are excited, such a "high
spot" must be admitted on its own merits as weird literature, no
matter how prosaically it is later dragged down. The one test of
the really weird is simply this—whether or not there be excited in
the reader a profound sense of dread, and of contact with unknown spheres and powers; a subtle attitude of awed listening, as
if for the beating of black wings or the scratching of outside shapes
and entities on the known universe's utmost rim. And of course,

the more completely and unifiedly a story conveys this atmosphere, the better it is as a work of art in the given medium. ...

Edgar Allan Poe

In the eighteen-thirties occurred a literary dawn directly affecting not only the history of the weird tale, but that of short fiction as a whole; and indirectly moulding the trends and fortunes of a great European aesthetic school. It is our good fortune as Americans to be able to claim that dawn as our own, for it came in the person of our most illustrious and unfortunate fellow-countryman Edgar Allan Poe. Poe's fame has been subject to curious undulations, and it is now a fashion amongst the "advanced intelligentsia" to minimize his importance both as an artist and as an influence; but it would be hard for any mature and reflective critic to deny the tremendous value of his work and the persuasive potency of his mind as an opener of artistic vistas. True, his type of outlook may have been anticipated; but it was he who first realized its possibilities and gave it supreme form and systematic expression. True also, that subsequent writers may have produced greater single tales than his; but again we must comprehend that it was only he who taught them by example and precept the art which they, having the way cleared for them and given an explicit guide, were perhaps able to carry to greater lengths. Whatever his limitations, Poe did that which no one else ever did or could have done; and to him we owe the modern horror-story in its final and perfected state.

Before Poe the bulk of weird writers had worked largely in the dark; without an understanding of the psychological basis of the horror appeal, and hampered by more or less of conformity to certain empty literary conventions such as the happy ending, virtue rewarded, and in general a hollow moral didacticism, acceptance of popular standards and values, and striving of the author to obtrude his own emotions into the story and take sides with the partisans of the majority's artificial ideas. Poe, on the other hand, perceived the essential impersonality of the real artist; and knew that the function of creative fiction is merely to express and interpret events and sensations as they are, regard-

less of how they tend or what they prove — good or evil, attractive
or repulsive, stimulating or depressing, with the author always
acting as a vivid and detached chronicler rather than as a teacher,
sympathizer, or vendor of opinion. He saw clearly that all phases
of life and thought are equally eligible as subject matter for the
artist, and being inclined by temperament to strangeness and
gloom, decided to be the interpreter of those powerful feelings
and frequent happenings which attend pain rather than pleasure,
decay rather than growth, terror rather than tranquility, and
which are fundamentally either adverse or indifferent to the tastes
and traditional outward sentiments of mankind, and to the health,
sanity, and normal expansive welfare of the species.

Poe's spectres thus acquired a convincing malignity possessed
by none of their predecessors, and established a new standard of
realism in the annals of literary horror. The impersonal and
artistic intent, moreover, was aided by a scientific attitude not
often found before; whereby Poe studied the human mind rather
than the usages of Gothic fiction, and worked with an analytical
knowledge of terror's true sources which doubled the force of his
narratives and emancipated him from all the absurdities inherent
in merely conventional shudder-coining. This example having
been set, later authors were naturally forced to conform to it in
order to compete at all; so that in this way a definite change began to affect the main stream of macabre writing. Poe, too, set a
fashion in consummate craftsmanship; and although today some
of his own work seems slightly melodramatic and unsophisticated,
we can constantly trace his influence in such things as the main-
tenance of a single mood and achievement of a single impression
in a tale, and the rigorous paring down of incidents to such as
have a direct bearing on the plot and will figure prominently in
the climax. Truly may it be said that Poe invented the short story
in its present form. His elevation of disease, perversity, and decay to the level of artistically expressible themes was likewise
infinitely far-reaching in effect; for avidly seized, sponsored, and
intensified by his eminent French admirer Charles Pierre
Baudelaire, it became the nucleus of the principal aesthetic movements in France, thus making Poe in a sense the father of the
Decadents and the Symbolists.

Poet and critic by nature and supreme attainment, logician and philosopher by taste and mannerism, Poe was by no means immune from defects and affectations. His pretence to profound and obscure scholarship, his blundering ventures in stilted and laboured pseudo-humour, and his often vitriolic outbursts of critical prejudice must all be recognized and forgiven. Beyond and above them, and dwarfing them to insignificance, was a master's vision of the terror that stalks about and within us, and the worm that writhes and slavers in the hideously close abyss. Penetrating to every festering horror in the gaily painted mockery called existence, and in the solemn masquerade called human thought and feeling, that vision had power to project itself in blackly magical crystallisations and transmutations; till there bloomed in the sterile America of the thirties and forties such a moon-nourished garden of gorgeous poison fungi as not even the nether slopes of Saturn might boast. Verses and tales alike sustain the burthen of cosmic panic. The raven whose noisome beak pierces the heart, the ghouls that toll iron bells in pestilential steeples, the vault of Ulalume in the black October night, the shocking spires and domes under the sea, the "wild, weird clime that lieth, sublime, out of Space—out of Time"—all these things and more leer at us amidst maniacal rattlings in the seething nightmare of the poetry. And in the prose there yawn open for us the very jaws of the pit—inconceivable abnormalities slyly hinted into a horrible half-knowledge by words whose innocence we scarcely doubt till the cracked tension of the speaker's hollow voice bids us fear their nameless implications; daemoniac patterns and presences slumbering noxiously till waked for one phobic instant into a shrieking revelation that crackles itself to sudden madness or explodes in memorable and cataclysmic echoes. A Witches' Sabbath of horror flinging off decorous robes is flashed before us—a sight the more monstrous because of the scientific skill with which every particular is marshaled and brought into an easy apparent relation to the known gruesomeness of material life.

Poe's tales, of course, fall into several classes; some of which contain a purer essence of spiritual horror than others. The tales of logic and ratiocination, forerunners of the modern detective story, are not to be included at all in weird literature; whilst certain others, probably influenced considerably by Hoffmann,

possess an extravagance which relegates them to the borderline
of the grotesque. Still a third group deal with abnormal psychology and monomania in such a way as to express terror but not
weirdness. A substantial residuum, however, represent the literature of supernatural horror in its acutest form; and give their
author a permanent and unassailable place as deity and fountain-
head of all modern diabolic fiction. Who can forget the terrible
swollen ship poised on the billow-chasm's edge in *MS. Found in
a Bottle*—the dark intimations of her unhallowed age and
monstrous growth, her sinister crew of unseeing greybeards,
and her frightful southward rush under full sail through the ice
of the Antarctic night, sucked onward by some resistless devil-
current toward a vortex of eldritch enlightenment which must
end in destruction?

Then there is the unutterable *M. Valdemar,* kept together by
hypnotism for seven months after his death, and uttering frantic
sounds but a moment before the breaking of the spell leaves him
"a nearly liquid mass of loathsome, of detestable putrescence." In
the *Narrative of Arthur Gordon Pym* the voyagers reach first a
strange south polar land of murderous savages where nothing is
white and where vast rocky ravines have the form of titanic Egyptian
letters spelling terrible primal arcana of earth; and thereafter a
still more mysterious realm where everything is white, and where
shrouded giants and snowy-plumed birds guard a cryptic cataract
of mist which empties from immeasurable celestial heights into
a torrid milky sea. *Metzengerstein* horrifies with its malign hints
of a monstrous metempsychosis—the mad nobleman who burns
the stable of his hereditary foe; the colossal unknown horse that
issues from the blazing building after the owner has perished
therein; the vanishing bit of ancient tapestry where was shown
the giant horse of the victim's ancestor in the Crusades; the madman's wild and constant riding on the great horse, and his fear
and hatred of the steed; the meaningless prophecies that brood
obscurely over the warring houses; and finally, the burning of
the madman's palace and the death therein of the owner, borne
helpless into the flames and up the vast staircase astride the beast
he has ridden so strangely. Afterward the rising smoke of the
ruins takes the form of a gigantic horse. *The Man of the Crowd,*
telling of one who roams day and night to mingle with streams

of people as if afraid to be alone, has quieter effects, but implies nothing less of cosmic fear. Poe's mind was never far from terror and decay, and we see in every tale, poem, and philosophical dialogue a tense eagerness to fathom unplumbed wells of night, to pierce the veil of death, and to reign in fancy as lord of the frightful mysteries of time and space.

Certain of Poe's tales possess an almost absolute perfection of artistic form which makes them veritable beacon-lights in the province of the short story. Poe could, when he wished, give to his prose a richly poetic cast; employing that archaic and Orientalised style with jeweled phrase, quasi-Biblical repetition, and recurrent burthen so successfully used by later writers like Oscar Wilde and Lord Dunsany; and in the cases where he has done this we have an effect of lyrical phantasy almost narcotic in essence—an opium pageant of dream in the language of dream, with every unnatural colour and grotesque image bodied forth in a symphony of corresponding sound. *The Masque of the Red Death, Silence, a Fable,* and *Shadow, a Parable,* are assuredly poems in every sense of the word save the metrical one, and owe as much of their power to aural cadence as to visual imagery. But it is in two of the less openly poetic tales, *Ligeia* and *The Fall of the House of Usher*—especially the latter—that one finds those very summits of artistry whereby Poe takes his place at the head of fictional miniaturists. Simple and straightforward in plot, both of these tales owe their supreme magic to the cunning development which appears in the selection and collocation of every least incident. *Ligeia* tells of a first wife of lofty and mysterious origin, who after death returns through a preternatural force of will to take possession of the body of a second wife; imposing even her physical appearance on the temporary reanimated corpse of her victim at the last moment. Despite a suspicion of prolixity and topheaviness, the narrative reaches its terrific climax with relentless power. *Usher,* whose superiority in detail and proportion is very marked, hints shudderingly of obscure life in inorganic things, and displays an abnormally linked trinity of entities at the end of a long and isolated family history—a brother, his twin sister, and their incredibly ancient house all sharing a single soul and meeting one common dissolution at the same moment.

These bizarre conceptions, so awkward in unskilful hands, become under Poe's spell living and convincing terrors to haunt our nights; and all because the author understood so perfectly the very mechanics and physiology of fear and strangeness—the essential details to emphasize, the precise incongruities and conceits to select as preliminaries or concomitants to horror, the exact incidents and allusions to throw out innocently in advance as symbols or prefigurings of each major step toward the hideous denouement to come, the nice adjustments of cumulative force and the unerring accuracy in linkage of parts which make for faultless unity throughout and thunderous effectiveness at the climactic moment, the delicate nuances of scenic and landscape value to select in establishing and sustaining the desired mood and vitalising the desired illusion—principles of this kind, and dozens of obscurer ones too elusive to be described or even fully comprehended by any ordinary commentator. Melodrama and unsophistication there may be—we are told of one fastidious Frenchman who could not bear to read Poe except in Baudelaire's urbane and Gallically modulated translation—but all traces of such things are wholly overshadowed by a potent and inborn sense of the spectral, the morbid, and the horrible which gushed forth from every cell of the artist's creative mentality and stamped his macabre work with the ineffaceable mark of supreme genius. Poe's weird tales are *alive* in a manner that few others can ever hope to be.

Like most fantaisistes, Poe excels in incidents and broad narrative effects rather than in character drawing. His typical protagonist is generally a dark, handsome, proud, melancholy, intellectual, highly sensitive, capricious, introspective, isolated, and sometimes slightly mad gentleman of ancient family and opulent circumstances; usually deeply learned in strange lore, and darkly ambitious of penetrating to forbidden secrets of the universe. Aside from a high-sounding name, this character obviously derives little from the early Gothic novel; for he is clearly neither the wooden hero nor the diabolical villain of Radcliffian or Ludovician romance. Indirectly, however, he does possess a sort of genealogical connection; since his gloomy, ambitious and antisocial qualities savour strongly of the typical Byronic hero, who in turn is definitely an offspring of the Gothic Manfreds, Montonis, and Ambrosios. More particular qualities appear to be derived from the psychology of Poe himself, who certainly possessed much of the depression, sensitiveness, mad aspiration, loneliness, and extravagant freakishness which he attributes to his haughty and solitary victims of Fate.

"Ghosts and Ghost-Seeing"[1] :
Spiritualism in American Occult Fiction

by Howard Kerr

While [James Russell] Lowell and the literary comedians were laughing at spiritualism during its early years, other writers found its mediums, manifestations, and doctrines suitable for serious literary treatment. With its millennial tone and its attraction for reformers and community men of all sorts, and with its susceptibility to charges of demonism and infidelity, the movement became the object of serious social and religious satire. Questions of belief aside, it also offered a topical frame of reference for supernatural fiction, and its phenomena—rappings, spirit-writing, materialized hands, spectral guitar music—offered specific occult devices. Exploitation along these lines was perhaps limited by the polemical furor which accompanied the movement, and by the inanities which drew the ridicule of humorists. Yet by repeatedly bringing ghosts to public attention, spiritualism probably helped stimulate the general appetite for supernatural fiction (as would the work of the Society for Psychical Research toward the end of the century). The mediums

[1][Tayler Lewis,] "Editor's Table," *Harper's* VI (April 1853), 699. Lewis's editorial (ibid., pp. 699-703) distinguished between traditional "ghost stories" and spiritualistic "ghost-seeing."

themselves, especially attractive young seeresses like the Fox sisters and Cora Hatch, fit neatly into established patterns of Gothic romance simply by virtue of their human situation and puzzling talent, and as time passed they came to provide a focus for writers interested in exploring unusual states of consciousness. Even in the work of the most serious writer, however, there was always the possibility that spiritualism might provoke laughter.

Nathaniel Hawthorne was the first writer of note to make serious literary use of such material. Hawthorne's attitude toward spiritualism grew out of his feelings about the "strange science" of mesmerism. Accepting mesmeric clairvoyance as physiological fact, he distrusted its use as ethically dangerous and denied that it was in any way supernatural. He was especially repelled by mesmeric claims of spirit communication. In 1841 he warned his fiancée, Sophia Peabody, whose interest in the occult was always to trouble him, against "magnetic miracles" which promised glimpses of the afterlife. Whatever happened, he told her, was "the result of a material and physical, not of a spiritual influence. ... I should as soon think of seeking revelations of the future state in the rottenness of the grave."[2]

Despite his dislike of mesmerism, Hawthorne employed it profitably in *The House of the Seven Gables* (1851) and *The Blithedale Romance* (1852) as a source of the marvelous with both supernatural ambience and potentially rational explanation, and as one version of the unpardonable sin.[3] The magnetic trances of Alice Pyncheon and Priscilla in these romances were of the very spirit-seeking sort against which he had cautioned Sophia.[4] But though he often commented on spiritualism itself in his journals, he never dealt with it very extensively in his

[2] Nathaniel Hawthorne, *Passages from the American Note Books* (Boston, 1891), pp. 244-45.

[3] Randall Stewart, ed., *American Notebooks,* by Nathaniel Hawthorne (New Haven, 1932), pp. lxxiv-lxxvi.

[4] At almost the same time that Lowell was writing about the requests addressed to Mr. Knott's spirits to identify the culprit "Who picked the pocket of Seth Crane,/ Of Waldo precinct, State of Maine," Hawthorne described Matthew Maule's attempt to convert Alice Pyncheon's mind "into a kind of telescopic medium" through which he could "obtain a glimpse into the spiritual world" and thereby find out who had stolen the entire Waldo precinct from the Pyncheon

fiction.[5] Nonetheless his early rejection of the American "epoch of the rapping spirits" in *The House of the Seven Gables* and *The Blithedale Romance* anticipated the lengthier attacks soon to follow from religious and social satirists, and perhaps indicated some of the problems which the phenomena of spiritualism posed for the writer of occult fiction. Later, in Italy, he discovered spiritualistic materials which he could adapt to his own habitual literary patterns. These materials he transformed into appropriate Gothic decor in *The Marble Faun* (1860) and drew upon for central character relationships in two of his unfinished romances, *Doctor Grimshawe's Secret* (1882) and *The Dolliver Romance* (1876). At no time, however, was he anything but skeptical of the spirits.

Hawthorne's skepticism took almost humorous initial form in *The House of the Seven Gables.* It is possible that the subject came to his attention as he worked on the book in the fall and winter of 1850-51. Late in the narrative Clifford Pyncheon insisted to a fellow railroad-passenger that spirit-rappings, along with mesmerism and electricity, were "harbingers of a better era" of spirituality in human life: "These rapping spirits that little Phoebe told us of, the other day.... What are these but the messengers of the spiritual world, knocking at the door of substance? And it shall be flung wide open!" In Clifford's words Hawthorne accurately caught the millennial tone of mesmeric and spiritualistic prophets like Andrew Jackson Davis, the Poughkeepsie seer, who had predicted even before the first rappings of the Fox sisters that "the world will hail with delight the ushering in of that era when the interiors of men will be opened, and the spiritual communion will be established such as is now being enjoyed

family. It is clear from the internal evidence, however, that Alice's trance was mesmeric and not at all spiritualistic; Hawthorne made no effort to connect it with the rappings which Clifford Pyncheon mentioned as a novelty.

[5]The most complete record of Hawthorne's attitudes toward spiritualism will be found in Elizabeth Ruth Hosmer, "Science and Pseudo-Science in the Writings of Nathaniel Hawthorne" (Ph.D. diss.: University of Illinois, 1948), pp. 274-303. Under the heading of "spiritualism," however, the author included any kind of communication with spirits, such as those practiced by the Shakers and the mesmerists well before the coming of the Fox sisters and the spiritualistic movement.

by the inhabitants of Mars, Jupiter, and Saturn."[6] Clifford's vision and the bracketing of spiritualism with mesmerism (itself already established in the person of Holgrave as a characteristic enthusiasm of reformers) suggest that Hawthorne first viewed the rappings as a foolish addition to the pattern of contemporary utopianisms criticized in the book.[7] But the reply of Clifford's commonsensical listener, that he would "love to rap, with a good stick, on the empty pates of the dolts who circulate such nonsense," indicated that the movement did not yet disturb the author very deeply.

A year later, however, *The Blithedale Romance* made it clear that Hawthorne had grown disgusted with spiritualism and mesmerism alike. Clifford's millennial rhetoric became sinister (and more like that of the Poughkeepsie seer) when assigned to the evil mesmerist, Westervelt, who spoke "of a new era...that would link soul to soul, and the present life to what we call futurity, with a closeness that should finally convert both worlds into one great, mutually conscious brotherhood." And while setting the scene for the Veiled Lady's final trance, Hawthorne's narrator Coverdale suddenly launched into a harangue on the evils of the "epoch of the rapping spirits" which had since succeeded mesmerism:

> Alas, my countrymen, methinks we have fallen on an evil age! If these phenomena have not humbug at the bottom, so much the worse for us. What can they indicate, in a spiritual way, except that the soul of man is descending to a lower point than it has ever before reached while incarnate? We are pursuing a downward course in the eternal march, and thus bring ourselves into the same range with beings whom death, in requital of their gross and evil lives, has degraded below humanity! To hold intercourse with spirits of this order, we must stoop and grovel in some element more vile than earthly dust. These goblins, if they exist at all, are but the shadows of past mortality, outcasts, mere refuse-stuff, ad-

---

[6]Andrew Jackson Davis, *The Principles of Nature, Her Divine Revelations, and a Voice to Mankind*, 3rd ed. (New York, 1847), pp. 675-76; Frank Podmore, *Modern Spiritualism: A History and a Criticism* (London, 1902), I, 163.

[7]Like Clifford, Holgrave sensed "harbingers abroad of a golden era, to be accomplished in his own lifetime."...

judged unworthy of the eternal world, and, on the most favorable supposition, dwindling gradually into nothingness. The less we have to say to them the better, lest we share their fate!

Perhaps this passage was included to point out the contemporary relevance of the novel's mesmeric background. But Coverdale's alternative explanations of the spirits as either fraudulent or "mere refuse-stuff," to communicate with whom "we must stoop and grovel in some element more vile than earthly dust," suggest that Hawthorne was lecturing his readers in the same way that he had warned Sophia a decade earlier against mesmerism. Probably, therefore, Coverdale's harangue resulted from an associative overflow of Hawthorne's own irritated and fearful feelings about trafficking with spirits, whether mesmeric or spiritualistic. ...

Hawthorne's unwillingness or inability to utilize spiritualism as an important frame of reference for supernatural fiction appears to have been the rule rather than the exception among the writers of the 1850's. Although Orestes Brownson's *Spirit-Rapper* (1854) and Bayard Taylor's "Confessions of a Medium" (1860) presented supernatural interpretations of spiritualism as demonic in origin, they were largely polemical in intention. No doubt there were more Gothic thrillers in the rationalistic tradition of *The Mysteries of Udolpho* than Arthur Hasting's "Birchknoll: A New Ghost Story of Old Virginia" (1856)[8] or Mrs. Southworth's "Haunted Homestead" (1860),[9] in which frightening phenomena were discovered to result from human villainy or natural accident. Such tales were merely the melodramatic counterparts of Benjamin Shillaber and Herman Melville's comic records of spurious manifestations. But of the serious ghost-story, that branch of supernatural fiction dealing with the mysterious or terrifying return of the dead to the land of the living, there were fewer examples involving spiritual manifestations and mediums than one might expect.

This failure to exploit probably owed a great deal to the public image of spiritualism. Because of the polemical furor over the movement, few writers responded to it in a neutral enough way to use it for mystification and terror. The mood and doctrine of the

[8][Arthur Hastings,] "Birchknoll." *Harper's* XII (February 1856), 336-40.
[9]E.D.E.N. Southworth, *The Haunted Homestead and Other Nouvellettes, with an Autobiography of the Author* (Philadelphia. 1860), pp. 45-110.

séance also mitigated against such effects. The sessions presided over by the Fox sisters, for instance, seem to have been altogether mundane in atmosphere. Rather than trying to baffle or frighten their clients, the girls emphasized the wonderful naturalness of communication with the departed, annoying one observer by eating peanuts and whispering to the young men in attendance. Especially did the inanity which so often subjected spiritual manifestations to the ridicule of humorists render them unlikely as dramatic material for supernatural fiction. Leah Fish closed her sisters' public séances by singing "Hail, Columbia" to the rhythmic accompaniment of rappings.[10] There was "no poetry," said the *Knickerbocker,* in these "Modern Sorcerers" whose bewitched table danced out replies to questions "of such popular interest as the number of teeth at present tenanting the interior of Mrs. Hobbs's mother's head."[11] The theology of the rappers had the same effect: the essence of Judge Edmonds's revelation was that death was no longer a terrifying mystery; rather, it was every man's promotion to a higher stage of existence not unlike the earthly one. Discussing "ghosts and ghost-seeing" in *Harper's,* Tayler Lewis charged the movement with "naturalizing" rather than "cultivating the imagination, or enhancing its religious awe, which was always more or less the effect of the old ghostly tales. ..."[12] It was in this critical vein that Hawthorne, who had relied on Alice Pyncheon's ghostly harpsichord music as an occult motif in *The House of the Seven Gables* (1851), soon denounced "tables upset by invisible agencies...and ghostly music performed by jewsharps" as trivial demonism or humbug in *The Blithedale Romance* (1852).

Inevitably, of course, some writers did exploit spiritualism for supernatural effects, though not always successfully. For instance, at about the same time that Hawthorne was rejecting both magnetic trance and séance music, Herman Melville, in *Pierre; or, The Ambiguities* (1852), was dramatizing Isabel Banford's revelation of secret kinship to Pierre Glendinning in terms of mesmeric electricity and spiritual guitar music. Just as Phoebe

[10]"To All Our Readers and Correspondents," *Holden's Dollar Magazine* VI (September 1850), 573-74.

[11]"Modern Sorcerers," *Knickerbocker* XLIII (February 1854), 171.

[12][Tayler Lewis,] "Editor's Table," *Harper's* VI (April 1853), 699.

Pyncheon had responded to "a certain magnetic element" in Holgrave's nature, so Isabel felt Pierre's "glance of magnetic meaning." Likewise, after singing her chant of "Mystery! Mystery!" Isabel appeared to Pierre "to swim in an electric fluid; the vivid buckler of her brow seemed as a magnetic plate." Such mesmeric metaphors for emotional and sexual attraction were commonplace in fiction. Indeed, while Melville was writing *Pierre,* the mesmeric and potentially incestuous affinity between a betrothed couple unaware that they were brother and sister was treated so as to satisfy the *Knickerbocker's* standards of propriety in Caroline Cheesebrough's "Magnetic Influences" (1851).[13]

But Isabel was more than magnetic. Singing her wild chant to the accompaniment of a guitar played by the ghost of her wronged mother, while lightning flashed outside the window, she became a spiritual medium:

> "Hark now; thou shalt hear my mother's spirit"....the magical untouched guitar responded with a quick spark of melody.... Again, after a preluding silence, the guitar as magically responded as before....and again Pierre felt as in the immediate presence of the spirit. ... Pierre felt himself surrounded by ten thousand sprites and gnomes, and his whole soul was swayed and tossed by supernatural tides.

Isabel's mediumship added her mother's testimony to the story of her mysterious origin, and it spiritualized her hold on Pierre, defining her at first glance as possessing magical power. (Newton Arvin called her guitar a "Magical Instrument"[14] borrowed by the novelist from Gothic tradition.) Melville qualified this power, however, by observing that the "all but intelligent responsiveness of the guitar" seemed inexplicable "at the time." And by noting that "sparks quivered" on the metallic strings of the instrument as its chords sounded near an open window outside of which "heat-lightnings and ground-lightnings wove their wonderfulness," he suggested, with a less explicit ambiguity than Hawthorne might have employed, a natural electrical explanation as an

---

[13]Herbert Ross Brown, *The Sentimental Novel in America, 1789-1860* (Durham, N.C., 1940), pp. 184-91; Caroline Cheesebrough, "Magnetic Influences," *Knickerbocker* XXXVII (May 1851), 430-41.

[14]Newton Arvin, *Herman Melville* (New York, 1950), p. 235.

alternative to the spiritual one. (The father of Egeria Boynton, the medium of Howells's *Undiscovered Country,* was sadly to conclude that static electricity was the source of his daughter's powers.)

What Melville did, then, was to extend Hawthorne's treatment of mesmerism within a Gothic framework to include spiritualism. Whether he was wise in selecting a musical manifestation to enhance the "Mystery of Isabel" is another matter. Since the early days of the séance, the guitar had been the spirits' favorite instrument. E. W. Capron had told of exquisite guitar music "played by unseen hands" in *Singular Revelations* (1850), a work which reached a much wider audience than did *Pierre.* And any reader who recognized the spiritualistic nature of Isabel's mysterious chords might well have been inappropriately reminded of Capron's enthusiastic but hardly Gothic report that "on one occasion we were getting the guitar played by these unseen musicians, and were asked to sing several tunes, among which were 'Get Off the Track,' and 'The Old Granite State!'"[15] Not until he directed ironic laughter at rappers and demons alike four years later did Melville successfully control spiritualistic material by concentrating on the psychology of his narrator's response to the mysterious tickings in "The Apple-Tree Table."

More in the manner of Edgar Allan Poe was Ferdinand C. Ewer's "Eventful Nights of August 20th and 21st, 1854" (1854).[16] As he later explained in an analysis admittedly inspired by Poe's "Philosophy of Composition," Ewer selected the device of spiritual manifestations to lend topical interest to the narrative of a soul's passage "through the gates of death and into the regions beyond." Ewer's narrator told of having been summoned to the deathbed of John F. Lane, a spiritualist who before dying was told by the spirits that as a supreme test he himself would communicate with the narrator from the next world. Following Lane's agonized passing, the clammy fingers of his corpse seized the narrator's hand and pencil to describe spiritland as "a long grand, misty,

[15]E. W. Capron and H. D. Barron, *Singular Revelations: Explanation and History of the Mysterious Communion with Spirits,* 2nd ed. (Auburn, N.Y., 1850), p. 73.

[16]The story was reprinted as part of F. C. Ewer, *The Eventful Nights of August 20th and 21st, 1854; and How Judge Edmonds Was Hocussed; or, Fallibility of "Spiritualism" Exposed* (New York, 1855), pp. 19-58.

undulating arch-way towards a *harmony,* as it were, of far-off
music." After two nights of such written communications, Lane's
body suddenly came awake to cry out loud, in horror, that his
spirit was being transported into another realm beyond the
spirit world, and that further communication would be impossible. "A whole universe was between us," said the narrator.
Aware that he would be attacked as "one of the insane dupes of
the spiritual rappers," he made the incident public out of a sense
of duty.

With the ghastly writing and speaking of Lane's corpse, Ewer's
tale reflected the interest taken by writers of sensational thrillers
and speculative science-fiction alike in the possibility of post-
mortem revivification (a possibility perhaps realized by the
spiritualists themselves with the "materializations" of the 1870's).
Indeed, with its charnel-house horror and pseudoscientific cir-
cumstantiality, "The Eventful Nights" evidently reminded some
readers that Poe had drawn a grisly picture of the results of mesmeric interference with the physical processes of death in "The
Facts in the Case of M. Valdemar" (1844), for Ewer was later at
some pains to deny any such indebtedness. His tale also bore
some resemblance to William North's imitation of Poe, "The
Living Corpse" (1853).[17] Most such fiction, of course, bobbed
somewhere in the wake of *Frankenstein.* Although the anonymous
author of *Zillah, the Child Medium* (1857)[18] said that his aim was
simply to report his own observations of spiritualism "in the form
of a domestic story," his climax was the satanic attempt of an insane scientific medium to recall life to the naked limbs of the dead
Zillah by means of the magnetic touch of his hand.

Questions about the nature of consciousness were sometimes
raised by such stories. The lapse of Ewer's John F. Lane into
eternal silence two nights after his death, for instance, may have
reflected the physiological problem of how long, if at all, the
brain goes on functioning after death. Ambrose Bierce's ironic
hypothesis of a hanged man's fleeting illusion of continued life
in "An Occurrence at Owl Creek Bridge" (1891)[19] would considerably shorten this period of "post-mortem consciousness."

[17][William North,] "The Living Corpse," *Putnam's* I (January 1853). 32-39.
[18]*Zillah, the Child Medium: A Tale of Spiritualism* (New York, 1857).
[19]Ambrose Bierce, *Tales of Soldiers and Civilians* (New York, 1891), pp. 21-39.

S. Weir Mitchell treated the ethical complications of restoring consciousness to a dead murderer with a quite unspiritualistic blood-pump in "Was He Dead?" (1870),[20] one of the more thoughtful tales of the kind. Mitchell had already dealt humorously with a similar theme in "The Case of George Dedlow" (1866),[21] using a spiritualistic hyperbole to explore one aspect of the human nervous system's subjectivity. As a medical man Mitchell had been intrigued during the Civil War by amputees' claims that they retained the sensations of their lost limbs. When his George Dedlow asked at a séance if his amputated legs were present in spirit, so lifelike a feeling of their existence came over him that he astonished the medium's other customers by walking about the room for a moment on his invisible limbs. The psychological point of the tale was evidently missed by the spiritualists, however, for according to Mitchell they were happy to accept George Dedlow's case as a real one when they read about it in the *Atlantic.*[22]

Even more Poe-like than Ewer's "Eventful Nights" itself was its success as a literary hoax. Neither Lane's experiences in the spirit world nor his revivified body owed anything to orthodox spiritualism. Indeed, for spirits to vanish so quickly into a realm of silence was inconsistent with the possibility of continued séance communication. Nonetheless Ewer's imitation of sincere accounts of spiritual manifestations was authentic enough to fool Judge John W. Edmonds. For when Ewer disingenuously sent the Judge a copy of the first part of the story in his San Francisco magazine, *The Pioneer,* Edmonds reprinted it in *The Christian Spiritualist* as a genuine report of spiritual intercourse. To Edmond's inquiry about further communications from Lane's spirit, Ewer responded only with the issue of *The Pioneer* containing the second half of the story. But in reprinting this second part, Edmonds appended additional messages which he, too, had received

[20][S. Weir Mitchell] "Was He Dead?" *Atlantic Monthly* XXV (January 1870), 86-102. See H. Bruce Franklin's introduction to the story in *Future Perfect: American Science Fiction of the Nineteenth Century* (New York, 1966), pp. 218-20.

[21][S. Weir Mitchell,] "The Case of George Dedlow," *Atlantic Monthly* XVIII (July 1866), 1-11.

[22]S. Weir Mitchell, *The Autobiography of a Quack and The Case of George Dedlow* (New York, 1900), P. x.

from the spirit of John F. Lane. Ewer's ironic disclosure of Edmonds's mistake embarrassed the spiritualists when it appeared
in the *New York Herald*. The Judge replied publicly, admitting
that he had been "fool enough to receive as true" a narrative
signed by Ewer, and stating that long experience as a criminal
judge had taught him "something of the degradation to which the
influence of evil passions, and a perverted education, may sink
the fairest-seeming among us." A letter to the *New York Daily
Chronicle* came to his rescue by pointing out that a military officer
named John F. Lane had committed suicide in 1836: "*There,*
Messrs. Editors, is a verifiable, genuine 'John F. Lane,' and no
mistake. When Judge Edmonds summoned the spirit of 'J. F. L.'
who is authorized to say that the genuine John did not respond?"
Ewer had the last word, however, in a volume entitled *The Eventful Nights of August 20th and 21st, 1854; and How Judge Edmonds Was Hocussed; or, Fallibility of "Spiritualism" Exposed*
(1855). From his discussion of the tale's composition it seems clear
that Ewer's first thought was to write a topically interesting ghost
story, and that not until it had been printed did he see its humorous possibilities. But nowhere better illustrated was the thin line
separating the supernatural from the ludicrous potential of spiritualistic literary materials.

The Occult in Later Victorian Literature

by John R. Reed

In addition to utilizing uncanny subject matter in their writings, many Victorian authors were familiar with mesmerism, spiritualism, and other versions of occult study. The Tennyson family is an example. Mary Tennyson was devoted to spiritualism through most of her life. At the time of Arthur Hallam's death she claimed to have seen an apparition that she took to be that of her brother's friend. Frederick Tennyson began to entertain spiritualist beliefs from the 1840s and eventually became a convinced advocate.[1] Alfred himself was curious about, if never convinced by, spiritualist thought. His poetry continually reveals a lively interest in the supernatural. *In Memoriam* records his speculations on survival after death and the relationship of the living to the dead as he speaks of "spiritual presentiments" wishing for Hallam's spirit to return to earth. Later, in "Aylmer's Field," the character Leolin wakes from sleep to respond, without understanding his act, to a preternatural call from his beloved Edith, and the poet wonders, "Star to star vibrates light: may soul to soul/ Strike through a finer element of her own?/ So, from afar, touch us at once?" "Demeter and Persephone" contains a simile comparing Persephone's manner of appearing before her mother to the likeness of a dying man's appearance to a far-off friend. And "The Ring" concerns the actual interference of a

[1]See Sir Charles Tennyson's, "The Somersby Tennysons," *Victorian Studies Christmas Supplement* (December, 1963).

spirit in the lives of its relations. A. P. Sinnett listed many other poems of Tennyson's as occult works, considering himself most suited to interpret them. "I am the better able to accomplish this," Sinnett wrote in 1920, "because I have had several recent opportunities of discussing the subject with the great poet himself, now, of course, in life on a higher plane of existence."[2] Tennyson may not have been an occultist, nor the latest reincarnation of a spirit who had led earlier lives as Virgil, Omar Khayyam, Dante and Spenser, as Sinnett claimed, but he did understand a good deal about occult thought and did not hesitate to make use of it in his poetry. Moreover, if he was not a spiritualist, he clearly had not given up belief in the possibility of a spiritual existence beyond the grave.

Robert Browning, too, maintained a faith in the reality of the spirit, though he remained unconvinced of spiritualism. His wife, however, was for a long time persuaded of its validity particularly because of the medium, Daniel Dunglas Home. "She was more and more convinced that the world was on the verge of a great revelation; that the widespread aliveness to the supernatural was a reaction from the materialism of the age."[3] She was disillusioned, though, by the fraudulent impositions of Mrs. Sophia Eckley, in whom she had believed. The circle in Florence, with whom the Brownings were friendly, also exhibited varying degrees of interest in spiritualism. Hiram Powers, James Jackson Jarves and Seymour Stocker Kirkup being enthusiastic, while Robert Lytton and Thomas Adolphus Trollope remained somewhat skeptical.[4]

William Bell Scott claimed to be familiar with the "shop filled with alchymical [*sic*] and astrological books and other related works, described by Bulwer in the introduction to" *Zanoni,* and he saw it and the club attended by some of his artistic friends and devoted to what he called "scientific superstition"—some of the members were engaged in a search for the *elixir vitae*—as signs of an interest in the occult in the first half of the nineteenth cen-

[2]A. P. Sinnett, *Tennyson an Occultist as His Writings Prove* (London, 1920), pp. 6-7.

[3]Katherine H. Porter, *Through a Glass Darkly. Spiritualism in the Browning Circle* (Lawrence, 1958), p. 46.

[4]See Porter and also Aurelia Brooks Harlan's *Owen Meredith: A Critical Biography of Robert, First Earl of Lytton* (New York, 1946).

tury.[5] Scott himself did not credit spiritualism, but he asserted that Rossetti had, and he told a story of Holman Hunt's encounter with what he supposed was the devil to illustrate the belief, among intelligent men, in the supernatural.[6] Richard Burton was very superstitious and maintained an interest in alchemy and spiritualism. Like Tennyson and Dickens, he was a capable hypnotist at a time when hypnotism was associated with the concept of animal magnetism formulated by Mesmer and later Count Puysegur. Burton's wife believed in gypsy horoscope predictions of future events and credited telepathic communication and hypnotism over long distances.[7] Laurence Oliphant offered a mystical substitute for traditional religion in its dogmatic form in the peculiar conclusion to *Piccadilly* (1866), and later, in his autobiographical *Episodes in a Life of Adventure, or, Moss from a Rolling Stone* (1887), he explained what moved him to withdraw from a life of politics and public events and devote himself to researches into "the more hidden laws which govern human action and control events."

> I had long been interested in a class of psychic phenomena which, under the names of magnetism, hypnotism, and spiritualism, have since been forcing themselves upon public attention, and had even been conscious of these phenomena in my own experience, and of the existence of forces in my own organism which science was utterly unable to account for, and therefore turned its back upon, and regulated to the domain of the unknowable.[8]

Naturally there was a good deal of debate in the periodical literature of the time about spiritualism, dreams and the supernatural. Although Dickens published articles critical of, and even mocking spiritualist pretensions in *Household Words* and *All the Year Round,* he also published stories based upon the supernatural in the latter journal, including his own tale, "The Haunted House." If *Blackwood's Edinburgh Magazine* con-

[5]William Bell Scott, *Autobiographical Notes of the Life of William Bell Scott and Notices of his Artistic and Poetic Circle of Friends 1830 and 1882,* ed. W. Minto, 2 vols. (New York, 1892), 1, p. 118.

[6]Ibid., 2, pp. 66, 231.

[7]Fawn M. Brodie, *The Devil Drives: A Life of Sir Richard Burton* (New York, 1967), p. 136.

[8]Laurence Oliphant, *Episodes in a Life of Adventure, or, Moss from a Rolling Stone* (New York, 1887), pp. 342-43.

sidered spiritualism as anti-Christian in "Spiritual Manifestations," the *Cornhill Magazine* printed Robert Bell's favorable account of spiritualism, "Stranger Than Fiction," which Thackeray defended.[9] The subject was clearly of interest to the general public and among literary people. That interest manifested itself as a literary convention in the later nineteenth century in England.

Nineteenth-century British literature demonstrated a Gothic fascination for supernatural events, either in quasi-mystical works such as Maturin's *Melmoth, The Wanderer* (1820), or in shockers, such as the vampire novels from Polidori's *The Vampyre* (1819), through T. P. Prest's *Varney the Vampyre, or the Feast of Blood* (1847) and Sheridan Le Fanu's *Carmilla* (1871-72), to Bram Stoker's *Dracula* (1897). Most popular fiction exploited conventional forms of premonition, prevision, and other occult warnings and communications. Finally, there were poems such as Adelaide Proctor's "Unseen," which reminded their readers of the mysterious forces surrounding them and sometimes ing their experience; "though a veil of shadow hangs between/ That hidden life and what we see and hear,/ Let us revere the power of the Unseen,/ And know a world of mystery is near." Most references to the occult and supernatural were made in a Christian context. Major poets employed the convention of the supernatural without necessarily admitting a faith in occult experience. Thus Browning alludes to the occult in *Paracelsus* and describes a gypsy's mysterious power in "The Flight of the Duchess"; Rossetti employs occult elements in "Rose Mary";[10] and Tennyson utilized traditional occult devices in several poems, for example, in the prevenient sign that Annie misinterprets, and the aural sign Enoch experiences in the very popular *Enoch Arden*.

From the sixties on, the occult played a prominent part in literature, reflecting the growing interest in spiritualism and the supernatural. Popular interest in spiritualism coincided with a renewed fascination for sensational novels and marvellous romances, but the two interests should not be confused. Many

[9]See vol. 73 of *Blackwood's*, pp. 629-46 and *Cornhill* for 1860, but also an article "Spiritualism," in the same journal for June, 1863.

[10]See Clyde K. Hyder's "Rossetti's *Rose Mary:* A Study in the Occult," *Victorian Poetry* 1 (1963), pp. 197ff.

writers of romance wished to be associated with neither development, and many who had comfortably employed the conventions of the occult in their work, mocked the new attitudes. Browning, for example, wrote "Mr. Sludge, The Medium," designed to cut figures such as D. D. Home down to size, as well as the more obscure poem, "Mesmerism," which reads like a parody of circumstances in certain sensational novels of the time. Joseph Sheridan Le Fanu, for one, fashioned his career upon tales of the uncanny, and though he was familiar with the writings of Swedenborg and other occultists, he never accepted spiritualism.[11] George MacDonald was writing stories pertaining to the marvellous as early as *The Phantastes* (1858) and in the preface to *The Portent: A Story of the Inner Vision of the Highlanders, Commonly Called the Second Sight* (published periodically in 1860, in book form in 1864), he specifically designated his story as a romance, explaining that although it was "founded in the marvellous" it was "true to human nature and to itself." He clearly asserted that his story was not to be classed "with what are commonly called *sensation novels.*"

The Portent describes the special sensibilities of three persons: Duncan Campbell who can hear a warning of impending trouble; Lady Alice, who has the same ability; and Margaret, Duncan's old nurse, who is able to project her soul according to her will. Lady Alice's soul is also given to drifting away from her body; the greater part of her early life has consisted of a tranced existence by day modified by a nocturnal spiritual life. After Duncan and Lady Alice have discovered their mutual spiritual attraction (they may even, it is hinted, be reincarnated lovers), and have been separated by a clumsy plot device, to be rejoined later through old Margaret's powers, they marry and assume a normal existence. Only at this point is the traditional moral presented: "love was the gate to an unseen world infinitely beyond that region of the psychological in which we had hitherto moved; for this love was teaching us to love all men, and live for all men." (ch. 26)

MacDonald continued to employ what may be called occult and even mystical elements in later novels such as *David Elginbrod* (1863), where mesmerism plays an important part, and *Lilith*

---

[11]See S. M. Ellis, *Wilkie Collins, Le Fanu and Others* (London, 1931), p. 176.

(1895), in which a world on the other side of a mirror contains
Adam and his first wife, Lilith, a vampire-like creature who
fascinates the main character, Mr. Vane. Other writers were also
eager to offer sophisticated, not to say learned, amplifications
of the occult convention. In Joseph Henry Shorthouse's *John
Inglesant* (1880), an historical romance, set largely in Renaissance England and Italy, there is frequent reference to such subjects as mystical Platonism or Rosicrucianism. There are instances
of true prevision, and in one experience Inglesant actually sees
the future in a crystal ball. These, however, are little more than
trappings, for the novel's real concern was with spiritual matura-
tion.

The interest in spiritualism was as active in America as it was
in England. Prominent authors such as Hawthorne, Lowell,
Howells, James and Twain, wrote of spiritualism, though they
were largely hostile to the belief itself.[12] In England, there was
more of the traditionally supernatural, as MacDonald's works
indicate.

Even Thomas Hardy used conventional occult devices, as in
Tess of the d'Urbervilles, where the sound of an evil ghostly
coach is perceivable only to true d'Urbervilles. Rudyard Kipling's tales of the uncanny, such as "The Phantom Rickshaw"
and "The Mark of the Beast," are, despite Kipling's interest in
spiritualism, largely conventional, while "My Own True Ghost
Story" is a takeoff on ghost stories. But conventions of this sort
gradually yielded to more sophisticated spiritualist approaches
in fiction. Ephemeral works such as the American, Elizabeth
Stuart Phelps' *The Gates Ajar* (1869) or Mrs. Adeline Whitney's
Hitherto (1869), prepared the way for more accomplished
writers like Mrs. Oliphant.

Underlying all of Mrs. Oliphant's stories of the Seen and Un-
seen was the desire to affirm the existence of a transcendental,
Christian creator and the immortality of the soul against the in-
creasing materialism and estheticism of her time. In 1880, Mrs.
Oliphant published *A Beleaguered City, Being a Narrative of
Certain Events in the City of Semur, in the Department of the
Haute Bourgogne. A Story of the Seen and the Unseen.* In this

---

[12]See Kerr for a full treatment of the literary manifestations of spiritualism
in nineteenth-century America.

graceful fable, the city of Semur is occupied by a ghostly, oppressive darkness. Unseen visitants force the city's inhabitants to leave. When the mayor, Martin Dupin, and the local priest venture into the city, they encounter the visionary Paul Lecamus, who alone has been permitted to remain conscious among the occupying spirits. Lecamus records his experiences, explaining that the visitants identified themselves as spirits of the city's dead who have returned out of love to teach its populace. Lecamus had always been interested in the mysterious and the unseen, but particularly since losing the wife he loved deeply. Here, as in other works of the time, love interrupted by death leads to a conviction of the reality of another life. It is yearning toward the life hereafter that enables Lecamus to believe in, and to experience spiritual existence. When the spirits depart from Semur, Lecamus' spirit goes with them and he dies.

The reason for the return of the spirits of the dead is purposely left ambiguous, but their general motive may be assumed both from Dupin's acknowledgment that "the thirst for money and for pleasure has increased among us to an extent which I cannot but consider alarming," (ch. 1) and from the ghostly "Sommation" placarded on the cathedral door, declaring "Go! leave this place to us who know the true signification of life." (ch. 2) Although this ghostly experience draws the community together and revives its religious faith, the agnostic Dupin, himself much moved by the mysterious events, sadly reports that the effects have not been lasting and the "wonderful manifestation which interrupted our existence has passed absolutely as if it had never been." (ch. 10) Mrs. Oliphant expressed both hope and dismay regarding human faith and the influence of the unseen. In *A Beleaguered City,* she was not merely exploiting a public taste for the marvellous and uncanny, for she felt a serious desire to revitalize religious emotion. There is a marked difference between this kind of uncanny tale and earlier Gothic novels. Though less intellectual, and less adept, Mrs. Oliphant's tale is in the tradition of Bulwer-Lytton's supernatural stories, rather than those of Le Fanu....

In 1886, two novels appeared that are representative of the directions that the occult convention took late in the century. H. Rider Haggard's *She* appeared serially in *The Graphic*. He had written the novel during February and March of 1886 in a little over six weeks and the book was a smashing best-seller from the start.[13] Haggard himself was interested in the supernatural and the tale came easily. He considered himself attuned to the spiritual, read Oliver Lodge's books on psychic research, studied Eastern religions, corresponded with individuals who believed in mystical experience and followed the activities of the Psychical Research Society. Haggard came to believe in reincarnation, finding it a sufficient explanation of the mystery of life and death. The rejuvenation theme itself was not unusual in English literature, and given Haggard's interests, it is not surprising that he used it in *She;* also, in keeping with conventional use, he associated true love with the eternal spirit.[14] Haggard continued to employ similar occult material in later novels, including the sequels to *She* and the late novel, *Love Eternal* (1918), but *She* remained the classic. The basic plot of the novel is simple. Leo Vincey is a reincarnation of Kallikrates, an ancient Egyptian. With his guardian, Ludwig Horace Holly, Leo goes to seek a strange land in Africa where his ancestor died at the hands of a mysteriously powerful white woman. At the ancient city of Kôr they encounter the irresistible, but cruel and violent Ayesha who has waited thousands of years for Kallikrates' return and now wishes to make his present physical embodiment as enduring as her own, but in the attempt she herself is reduced to dust. Both Leo and Holly become wanderers haunted by Ayesha's beauty.

One of Haggard's favorite novelists was Bulwer-Lytton, and much of *She* bears resemblance to both *Zanoni* and *A Strange Story.* In *Zanoni* simple faith was favorably contrasted to a lust for knowledge; similarly, Haggard writes that "Truth is veiled, because we could no more look upon her glory than we can upon the sun. It would destroy us. Full knowledge is not for man as man is here, for his capacities, which he is apt to think so great, are indeed but small." (ch. 10) Just as Zanoni discovers that physical immortality is not preferable to death, so Holly tells She that her offer of long life is nothing compared to what he anticipates; "the immortality to which I look, and which my faith doth promise to me," he says, "shall be free from the bonds

[13]Morton Cohen, *Rider Haggard: His Life and Works* (London, 1960), p. 97.
[14]Ibid., p. 111.

that here must tie my spirit down." (ch. 22) Ayesha says that the next life differs little, morally, from this one (a view presented as early as Swedenborg and echoed in such writers as Catherine Crowe and Mrs. Oliphant). Ayesha considers religions generally inclined to error because of their confidence in dogma. "Ah!" she exclaims, "if man would but see that hope is from within, and not from without—that he himself must work out his salvation! He is there, and within him is the breath of life and a knowledge of good and evil, as good and evil are to him." (ch. 17) Despite her intelligence, Ayesha is not wise enough for humility. Her name is borrowed from *A Strange Story,* where Ayesha is the loving companion of the radiantly handsome Margrave, whose attempt to achieve immortality is rebuked by spirits in the air. Haggard's She also fails in her desire for prolonged existence. As the moral Holly observes, "she opposed herself to the eternal law, and, strong though she was, by it was swept back into nothingness—swept back with shame and hideous mockery!" (ch. 26) Haggard made full use of supernatural and uncanny conventions, incorporating them in a confusedly affirmative view of traditional morality. Though *She* may be viewed as a thriller, it is also a serious expression of opinion regarding the unseen and the unknown.

The second highly successful novel dealing with the marvellous appearing in 1886 was Marie Corelli's *A Romance of Two Worlds.* If Haggard had been willing to consider features of spiritualism as proof of Christianity, Marie Corelli quite clearly distinguished her beliefs from anything related to what she called the craze for occultism or spiritualism. In her preface to a new edition of the novel, she asserted that her faith was based solely on Christ, and her answer to the yearning for a spiritual progress was love for God. Yet any reader of Corelli's novel might have been forgiven his confusion, since, although in the Prologue to the tale the narrator explains that her experiences offer evidence of the real existence of the supernatural around us—evidence she expects will be disbelieved in this age of materialistic skepticism— actually her supernaturalism sounds more hermetic and occult than strictly Christian.

The nameless narrator is a young *improvatrice* suffering from a peculiar physical malaise. From a friend she receives an elixir that reveals to her that her malady is spiritual. She is directed to the sage Heliobas, who undertakes not only to cure her, but to educate her as well. Heliobas promotes an Electric Creed of Christianity, based on the notion, later verified by the narrator's spiritual journey, that divinity is a sphere within a ring of light from which electricity extends throughout the universe. That electricity is of two kinds — external, bound by universal law, and internal.

> Internally it is the germ of a soul or spirit, and is placed there to be either cultivated or neglected as suits the will of man. It is inde-structible; yet, if neglected, it remains always a germ; and, at the death of the body it inhabits, goes elsewhere to seek another chance of development. If, on the contrary, its growth is fostered by a per-severing resolute WILL, it becomes a spiritual creature, glorious and supremely powerful, for which a new, brilliant, and endless existence commences when its clay chrysalis perishes. (ch. 7)

When, through Heliobas' power, the narrator journeys to the spiri-tual realm, she learns what Heliobas later relates more prosaically: God's likeness in man is an electric flame which may be fostered or neglected; Christ came to earth not as a sacrifice, but to estab-lish an electric communication (compared to a telegraph cable) between men and the central sphere; the soul may progress or regress after physical death; and also, "this world is *the only spot in the Universe* where His existence is actually questioned and doubted." (ch. 14)

The narrator also learns, through her acquaintance with Casimir Heliobas and his lovely sister, Zara, that each soul has a twin soul either embodied in flesh or not. Heliobas' spiritual mate is Azúl, who watches over him. Zara's unearthly lover comes to possess her finally in a bolt of lightning, freeing her from the restrictive flesh. With this knowledge to fortify her, and increas-ing electrical powers to both disturb and console her, the narrator goes on to lead a satisfying earthly life, concluding her tale with a plea to her readers to think seriously about their own lives, to consider what Progress really means, and not to lightly deny God. It is, she asserts, a universe powered by love in which our wills are free.

Corelli referred to the uncanny and the life beyond death in later works such as *The Soul of Lilith* (1892) and *The Sorrows of Satan* (1895). The latter novel tells of Geoffrey Tempest's temptation by the devil in the form of one Rimanez. After a prolonged struggle, Tempest frees himself from the devil by choosing God instead. This novel was praised by defenders of Christianity. Eileen Bigland, in her biography of Corelli, quotes from a certain Father Ignatius' sermon delivered at Portman Rooms in Baker Street, who thanked God for the book and declared "*The Sorrows of Satan* is flung down into the midst of English society, as it is constituted at present, as an heroic challenge to that society and to the Church."[15] Corelli's supernatural novels were almost evangelical in their spirit and did constitute challenges, as Father Ignatius asserted. But other writers could be equally positive, yet less aggressive, and more sentimental in their use of the occult convention.

In *Peter Ibbetson* (1892), George du Maurier relates the history of a man who comes to live a real life in dreams with the woman he loves. In the disembodied world of dreams, their spirits meet, controlling time and space. The lovers marvel at their shared gift, "penetrated to the very heart's core by a dim sense of some vast, mysterious power, latent in the subconsciousness of man—unheard of, undreamed of as yet, but linking him with the Infinite and the Eternal." (ch. 5) When Peter's beloved dies, the dream world changes; whereas they had enjoyed perennial youth, now Peter is left old and alone. But Mimsey is able to return to him from beyond death to tell Peter they will unite with the One when he joins her in the next life. She tells him that the foundation of the next life is earthly existence and that earth is the most favored planet. "Like many who lived before me," she admits, "I cannot prove—I can only affirm." (ch. 6) But what she affirms is that "Nothing is lost—nothing," of human experience, though the cause of all being remains inscrutable. There is continual advance without end, she assures Peter and leaves him with the promise *"that all will be well for us all, and of such a kind that all who do not sigh for the moon will be well content."* (ch. 6)

George du Maurier also wrote *The Martian* (1897) as well as the amazingly popular *Trilby* (1894), which exploited another aspect of occult interest, mesmerism. In *Trilby*, the hypnotist,

[15]Eileen Bigland, *Marie Corelli: The Woman and the Legend. A Biography.* (London, 1953), p. 163.

Svengali, controls young Trilby's nature to such an extent that
she unknowingly leads two distinct and contradictory lives.
When Svengali dies and his power fades, Trilby also expires.
This relationship recalls George MacDonald's earlier novel,
David Elginbrod (1863), where the character, Euphra, is mes-
merized by an evil figure named Funkelstein, supposedly drawn
partly from a Pole named Zamoyski who was lecturing on "elec-
trobiology" in England at the time MacDonald wrote his story.[16]
But hypnotism had long been a familiar part of the occult convention, as seen in E. T. A. Hoffmann's tale *Der Magnetiseur,*
published in 1814.

Spiritualist or not, the convention of the occult was used largely
as a defense of religious belief among late-Victorian writers.
Early in the century, supernatural visitations and portents
abounded, but they served more often to arouse thrills than to
support a larger scheme of faith.[17] As the century proceeded,
several notable utilizations of the occult convention in fiction
indicated a change in literary approaches. Just as philosophical,
religious and "psychological" tracts were more ambitiously
examining the possibilities of the verification of the supernatural,
literary artists were learning to utilize old conventions in new or
more serious ways.

This force of serious conviction altered what might otherwise
have been mere sensational writing. In Bram Stoker's *Dracula*
(1897), the characters are appalled at the prospect of a deathless
being gradually accumulating knowledge and power, a dread
that had troubled Holly soon after experiencing Ayesha's power,
when he considered "what may not be possible to a being who,
unconstrained by human law, is also absolutely unshackled by a
moral sense of right and wrong." (*She,* ch. 18) Bulwer-Lytton
and Haggard wrote to scold an age that refused to believe in
mysteries which it could not explain; so in part, did Stoker. His
open-minded Professor Von Helsing, Count Dracula's true an-

[16]See Robert Lee Wolff, *The Golden Key: A Study of the Fiction of George
MacDonald* (New Haven, 1961), p. 401, n. 18.

[17]Devendra P. Varma mentions more than once in *The Gothic Flame,* that
Gothic fiction often treated tales in which poetic justice exhibited itself and
moral virtue triumphed. This is not entirely the same sort of scheme of faith
that I am referring to. ...

tagonist, is obliged to instruct his brilliant, but materialistic friend, Dr. John Seward, that there are things outside every day life that cannot be accounted for. "Do you not think," he asks, "that there are things which you cannot understand, and yet which are; that some people see things that others cannot?" He then criticizes science for Seward's attitude because "if it explain not, then it says there is nothing to explain." (ch. 14) Von Helsing concludes his argument abruptly. "My thesis is this: I want you to believe." "To believe what?" the puzzled Seward replies, and the doctor responds: "To believe in things that you cannot." (ch. 14) *Dracula* implicitly denounces its "sceptical and selfish" age; and the threat of "a spreading army of soulless Un-Dead" is, to some extent, a warning about a world peopled by materialistic, and therefore soulless men, unable to value life. Appropriately, Stoker has Dracula defeated by his own selfish purpose, for it is through his own volitional powers that his enemies are able to pursue and destroy him. Stoker continued to exploit supernaturalism in novels such as *The Mystery of the Sea* (1902), *The Jewel of Seven Stars* (1904) and *The Lair of the White Worm* (1911), but never approached the power of *Dracula* again.

The use of the occult by writers of romance provided an opportunity for yet another, similar utilization of the convention, as in Theodore Watts-Dunton's *Aylwin* (1898). For Watts-Dunton, as for many spiritualists, the spiritual was less divine than earthly. Aylwin is filled with secular superstitions, especially related to gypsies, who were customarily identified with the occult; it utilizes the ancient convention of a curse, but makes it plausible psychologically. Even Winifred Wynne's astonishing cure by magnetism Watts-Dunton defended as scientifically possible. But essentially the novel describes Henry Aylwin's progress from stern determinism to a new, open-minded and open-hearted acceptance of wonder and mystery in existence. His friend, D'Arcy, writes to him when his greatest ordeal is ended: "As Job's faith was tried by Heaven, so has your love been tried by the power which you call 'circumstance' and which Wilderspin calls 'the spiritual world.' All that death has to teach the mind and the heart of man you have learnt to the very full." (ch. 16)

What Henry learns is the spiritual power of love. The death

of a beloved is the greatest human tragedy and leads a man to supernaturalism in the desperate hope not to be separated forever.[18] Henry might have learned from his own father's history. Philip Aylwin had seen his first wife die and thereafter, prompted by desperate longing, became a mystic in a sect founded by Lavater, putting his convictions down in a book entitled *The Veiled Queen,* and believing himself in communication with his dead wife. But Henry despises superstition, and struggles to forge a way of life to contend with all-powerful Circumstance. His ordeal, as we have noted, brings him finally to a belief in mysteries beyond the ken of materialist philosophies.

Seeming to alter considerably, the occult convention had changed only slightly, though significantly, in the nineteenth century. It still was used to suggest the existence of another world affecting our own, but as the nineteenth century progressed, it came to have a more serious function in English literature. Oscar Wilde's delightful tale, "The Canterville Ghost" (1891), in which a respectably ancient ghost is driven to despair by an American family who purchase the estate he haunts and who refuse to be terrified by him, is a fine satire upon the kinds of sensational and popular ghost stories. But while many writers continued to employ the convention superficially, others based their fables upon the probable reality of the Unseen. Moreover, if earlier supernatural phenomena in literature were random and mainly ominous, by the end of the century such occurrences were largely benign and hopeful. With or without religious belief, many literary people exhibited some degree of faith in spiritualist revelations, and one of the greatest, W. B. Yeats, not only became a student of the occult and fashioned his own occult scheme, he married a medium, Georgie Hyde Lees, in 1917 and benefited thereafter from her skill.

This developing interest in the uncanny, and the modifications

---

[18]Novalis' religious susceptibilities, and concern for a life hereafter, were heightened by the loss of his fiancée, Sophie von Kühn. Tennyson's mind dwelt upon similar subjects after the death of Arthur Henry Hallam. This sense of loss appears as an important feature of Bulwer-Lytton's *A Strange Story,* and other fiction. Both Frederic Myers and Oliver Lodge were moved to investigations of the possibilities of life after death by their bereavements.

it occasioned in a traditional literary convention, indicates a powerful desire during the nineteenth century for some means of escape from a depressingly materialistic existence. Amice Lee, describing William Howitt's reaction against the spirit of his time, writes that "Howitt believed with all the vehemence of his nature that spiritualism militated against the fierce materialism of the age. Nothing seemed to matter except to get on and make money — money, that was all men cared for now. In the London streets, he said, the very air you breathed hummed with voices discussing 'Shares.'"[19] Time and again rationalist heroes, such as Bulwer-Lytton's Dr. Fenwick, Stoker's Dr. Seward, or Watts-Dunton's Henry Aylwin, when faced with inexplicable events, are obliged to recognize that there are powers beyond man's ability to comprehend or control. If the sense of such ominous powers had once been primarily associated with demonic forces which made acceptance of a secure social existence valuable and desirable, by the end of the century the Unknown had become an attractive intellectual magnet, promising an experience beyond the dull confinement of modern life, promising, in fact, a release from an existence which seemed drained of meaning and feeling. In novels such as *Zanoni* and *A Romance of Two Worlds,* the possibility of liberation from the flesh itself fulfilled the fantasy of absolute freedom of the mind. But perhaps du Maurier's Peter Ibbetson is the archetypal hero of this mode. Bound in the triple prison of an actual institution, meaningless modern life, and the flesh, he escapes by apparent madness, life in dreams, and the promise of an eternity of love. If the convention of the occult and uncanny continued, then, with its ghosts and marvels, it acquired a higher purpose as well, for it came to represent release from confinements which appeared, to many, more and more intolerable. The uncanny was an antidote to relentless materialism, it was a promise of love and fullness of feeling beyond the unfeeling mechanization of modern society. In this sense it was a form of social protest. At the same time it represented a metaphysical craving for the liberation of the mind from the statistical and measurable habits of the late nineteenth cen-

---

[19] Amice Lee, *Laurels and Rosemary: The Life of William and Mary Howitt* (London, 1955), p. 224.

tury. In this modification of a perennial literary convention, it is possible to see how subtle if not always skillful an artistic accommodation had taken place; and also how responsive to its society, and therefore revelatory of that society, such conventions can be.

Modern Ghosts

by Dorothy Scarborough

The ghost is the most enduring figure in supernatural fiction. He is absolutely indestructible.

...He appears as unapologetically at home in twentieth-century fiction as in classical mythology, Christian hagiology, medieval legend, or Gothic romance. He changes with the styles in fiction but he never goes out of fashion. He is the really permanent citizen of this earth, for mortals, at best, are but transients.... The ghost, like death, has all seasons for its own and there is no closed season for spooks. It is much the case now as ever that all the world loves a ghost, yet we like to take our ghosts vicariously, preferably in fiction. We'd rather see than be one.

One point of difference between the ghostly fiction of the past and of the present is in the matter of length. The Gothic novel was often a three- or four-decker affair in whose perusal the reader aged perceptibly before the ghost succeeded or was foiled in his haunting designs. There was obviously much more leisure on the part of spooks as well as mortals then than now. Consequently the ghost story of to-day is told in short-story form for the most part. Poe knew better than anybody before him what was necessary for the proper economy of thrills when he gave his dictum concerning the desirable length for a story, which rule applies more to the ghostly tale than to any other type, for surely there is needed the unity of impression, the definiteness of effect which only continuity in reading gives. The ghostly narrative that is too long loses in impressiveness. ...

The apparitions in later English fiction fall naturally into several distinct classes with reference to the reality of their appearance. There are the mistaken apparitions, there are the purely subjective specters, evoked by the psychic state of the percipients, and there are the objective ghosts, independent of the mental state of the witnesses, appearing to persons who are not mentally prepared to see them.

The mistaken ghost is an old form, for most of Mrs. Radcliffe's interesting apparitions belong to this class and others of the Gothic writers used subterfuge to cheat the reader. In the early romance there was frequently deliberate deception for a definite purpose, the ghosts with the histrionic temperament using a make-up of phosphorus, bones, and other contrivances to create the impression of unearthly visitation. Recent fiction is more cleverly managed than that. Rarely now does one find a story where the ghost-seer is deliberately imposed upon, for in most modern cases the mistake occurs by accident or misapprehension on the part of the percipient, for which nobody and nothing but his own agitation is responsible. ...

The subjective ghosts are legion in modern fiction. They are those evoked by the mental state of the percipients so that they become realities to those beholding them. The mind rendered morbid by grief or remorse is readily prepared to see the spirits of the dead return in love or with reproach. The apparitions in animistic beliefs, as in classical stories and Gothic romance, were usually subjective, born of brooding love or remorse or fear of retribution, appearing to the persons who had cause to expect them and coming usually at night when the beholders would be alone and given over to melancholy thought or else to troubled sleep. Shakespeare's ghosts were in large measure subjective, "selective apparitions." When Brutus asked the specter what he was, the awful answer came, "Thy evil genius, Brutus!" Macbeth saw the witches who embodied for him his own secret ambitions, and he alone saw the ghost of Banquo, because he had the weight of murder on his heart. ...

Objective ghosts are likewise very numerous in modern fiction. The objective spirits are those that, while they may be subjective on the part of the persons chiefly concerned, to begin with, are yet visible to others as well, appearing not only to those mentally prepared to see them but to others not thinking of such manifestations and even sceptical of their possibility. The objective ghosts have more definite visibility, more reality than the purely subjective spirits. They are more impressive as haunters. There is a plausibility, a corporeality about the later apparitions that shows their advance over the diaphanous phantoms of the past. ... In *The Four-fifteen Express*,[1] John Derringer's ghost is seen by a man that does not know he is dead, and who has not been thinking of him at all. The ghost reveals incontrovertible proof of his presence, even leaving his cigar-case behind him—which raises the question as to whether ghosts smoke in the hereafter in more ways than one. ...

Whether ghosts be mistaken, subjective or objective, their appearance has always elicited considerable interest on the part of humanity. Their substance of materialization, their bearing, dress, and general demeanor are matters of definite concern to those who expect shortly to become ghosts themselves. In some instances the modern ghost sticks pretty closely to the animistic idea of spirit material, which was that the shade was a sort of vapory projection of the body, intangible, impalpable, yet easily recognized with reference to previous personality. Chaucer describes some one as being "nat pale as a forpyned goost," which illustrates the conception in his day, and the Gothic specimen was usually a pallid specter, though Walpole furnished one robust haunter of gigantic muscle. Yet for the most part the Gothic ghosts were misty wraiths, through which the sword could plunge without resistance. They were fragile and helpless as an eighteenth-century heroine when it came to a real emergency, and were useful chiefly for frightening the guilty and consoling the innocent. ...

The Gothic ghost frequently walked forth as a skeleton, clad in nothing but his bones and a lurid scowl. Skeletons still perambulate among us, as in *The Messenger*, where the stripped-off mask shows a hideous skull.

> The skeleton burst from out the rotting robes and collapsed on the ground before us. From between the staring ribs and the grinning

[1]By Amelia B. Edwards.

teeth spurted a torrent of black blood, showering the shrinking grasses, and then the thing shuddered and fell over into the black ooze of the bog.

...But on the whole, though skeletons do appear in later fiction, the rattle of bones is not heard as often as in Gothic times.

Ghostly apparitions are more varied in form than in early times. The modern ghost does not require a whole skeleton for his purposes, but he can take a single bone and put the hardiest to flight with it. It is a dreadful thing to realize that a ghost can come in sections, which indefinitely multiplies its powers of haunting. F. Marion Crawford has a story of a diabolical skull, one of the most rabid revenge ghosts on record. A man has murdered his wife by pouring melted lead into her ear while she slept, in accordance with a suggestion from a casually told story of a guest. The dead woman's skull—the husband cut the head off for fear people would hear the lead rattle, and buried it in the garden— comes back to haunt the husband, with that deadly rattle of the lump of lead inside. The teeth bite him, the skull rolls up a hill to follow him, and finally kills him, then sets in to haunt the visitor who told the suggestive story.[2]...The revenge ghost in modern fiction frequently manifests itself in this form, mutilated or dismembered, each disfigurement of the mortal body showing itself in a relentless immortality and adding to the horror of the haunting. There seems to be no seat of ghostly mind or soul, for the body can perform its function of haunting in whole or in part, unaided by the head or heart, like a section of a snake that has life apart from the main body....

Ghosts of modern fiction are more convincing in their reality than the specters of early times. They are stronger, more vital; there seems to be a strengthening of ghostly tissue, a stiffening of supernatural muscle in these days. Ghosts are more healthy, more active, more alive than they used to be. There is now as before a strong resemblance to the personality before death, the same immortality of looks that is discouraging to the prospects of homely persons who have hoped to be more handsome in a future state. Fiction gives no basis for such hope. Peculiarities of appearance are carried over with distressing faithfulness to detail, each freckle, each wrinkle, each gray hair showing with the clear-

[2] *The Screaming Skull.*

ness of a photographic proof....Each minor disfigurement is retained, as the loss of the tooth in Crawford's screaming skull, the missing toe in Bierce's *Middle Toe of the Right Foot,*...and so forth. Nothing is neglected to make identification absolute in present tales of horror. ...

Another point of difference between the specters of to-day and those of the past is in the extension of their avenues of approach to us. Ghostly appeal to the senses is more varied now than in earlier times. The classical as well as the Gothic ghosts appealed in general only to the sight and hearing, as well as, of course, to the sixth sense that realizes the presence of a supernatural being. Ghosts were seen and heard and were content with that. But nowadays more points of contact are open to them and they haunt us through the touch, the smell, as well as sight and hearing.... In *The Haunted Hotel,*[3] the ghost manifests itself through the nostrils. In room number thirteen there is an awful stench for which no one can account, and which cannot be removed by any disinfectants. Finally when a woman especially sympathetic to a man mysteriously dead is put in the room, the ghost appears as a decaying head, floating near the ceiling and emitting an intolerable odor. *The Upper Berth*[4] tells of a strange, foul sea odor that infests a certain stateroom and that no amount of fumigating or airing will remove. ...

But it is through the sense of touch that the worst form of haunting comes. Seeing a supernatural visitant is terrible, hearing him is direful, smelling him is loathsome, but having him touch you is the climax of horror. This element comes in much in recent stories. The earlier ghosts seemed to be more reserved, to know their spectral place better, were not so ready to presume on unwelcome familiarities as those in later fiction, but spooks have doubtless followed the fashion of mortals in this easy, relaxed age and have become a shade too free in their manners. Of course, one remembers that crushing specter in Otranto castle that flattened the hapless youth out so effectually, and there are other instances less striking. But as a general thing the Gothic ghost was content to stand at a distance and hurl curses. Fortunately for our ancestors' nerves, he did not incline much to the

[3]By Wilkie Collins.
[4]By F. Marion Crawford.

laying on of hands. Modern ghosts, however, have not been taught to restrain their impulses and they venture on liberties that Radcliffian romance would have disapproved of. ...

Another point of contrast between the modern and the older ghosts is in the greater freedom enjoyed by those of to-day. The ghosts of our ancestors were weak and helpless creatures in the main and the Gothic specter was tyrannized over to such an extent that he hardly dared call his shade his own. The spook of to-day has acquired a latchkey and asserted his independence. He may have a local habitation but he isn't obliged to stay there. Now-a-days even the spectral women are setting up to be feminists and have privileges that would have caused the Gothic wraiths to swoon with horror. Ghosts are not so sensitive to the barometer now as they used to be, nor do they have such an active influence over the weather as did the Gothic phantoms. They do not need a tempest for their materialization nor a supernatural play of lightning for their wild threats, and comparatively few storms occur in later fiction. Yet there is certainly no lessening of the ghostly thrill in consequence. ...

Ghostly psychology is a fascinating study. The development of spectral personality is one of the evident facts gained from a historical survey of supernatural fiction. The modern ghost has more individuality, more distinctiveness, in the main, than his forbears. The ghosts of medievalism, of ancient superstition, and the drama were for the most part pallid, colorless beings in character as in materialization. The ancient ghosts were more mournful than the moderns, since the state of the dead in early times was by no means enviable. The most one could hope for then was Hades, while the spirits who hadn't been buried couldn't find entrance even there but were forced by relentless spectral police to keep forever moving. The Christian religion furnishes a more cheerful outlook, so in later manifestations the gloom is considerably lightened. Yet even so the Gothic ghosts were morbid, low-minded specters not much happier than the unlucky wights they felt it their business to haunt. ...For the most part the later ghosts are something more than merely unhappy spirits. They are more positive, more active, more individualistic, too philosophical to waste time in useless grieving. ...

The ghosts that are actively vicious are the most vivid and

numerous in later fiction. The spirits of evil seem to have a terrible cumulative force, being far more maleficent than the earlier ones, and more powerful in carrying out their purposes. Every aspect of supernaturalism seems to be keyed up to a higher pitch of terror. Evil seems to have a strangely greater power of immortality over that of good, judging from the proportion employed in modern fiction. Has evil so much more strength of will, so much more permanence of power that it lives on through the years and centuries, while good deeds perish with the body? It would appear so from fiction. The ghosts of good actions do not linger round the abode of the living to any noticeable extent, but evil deeds are deathless. We have many stories of places and persons haunted by the embodied evil of the past, but few by the embodied good. The revenge ghosts outnumber the grateful dead by legions.

Modern specters have a more complex power than the old. They are more awful in their import, for they haunt not merely the body, but the soul. The wicked spirits will to work dreadful harm to the soul as well as the body, and drive the victim to spiritual insanity, seeking to damn him for the life everlasting, making him, not merely their victim, but through eternity their co-worker in awful evil. The victim of the vampire, for instance, who dies as a result of the attack, has to become in his turn a loathsome vampire to prey on other souls and bodies. Blackwood's Devil-worshipers seek to kill the soul as well as the body of their victim. The deathlessness of evil is shown in Lytton's[5] and in many of Blackwood's stories, as where the psychic doctor says to a man, "You are now in touch with certain violent emotions, passions, purposes, still active in this house, that were produced in the past by some powerful and evil personality that lived here."...

Ambrose Bierce's stories are in many instances remarkable examples of this psychic horror. *The Death of Halpin Frazer* has a touch of almost unbearable dreadfulness. Frazer is assaulted by an evil spirit in a wood at night and choked to death, the spirit inhabiting the dead body of the man's own mother who has idolized him. His dead mother's face, transfixed with diabolical hate, is thrust upon him, and the loved hands that have caressed him

[5]*The Haunters and the Haunted.*

strangle him. This is similar to the situation of an evil spirit occupying the body of a loved dead mother in *The Mummy's Tale*, by Elliot O'Donnell. Bierce's stories beat upon the mind like bludgeons and his morbid plots are among the most dreadful in our literature. ...There is more than one writer of modern ghostly fiction of whom it might be said that "his soul is open on the Hell side.". ...

As may be seen,...the ghost has made perceptible progress in psychology. The modern apparition is much more complex in personality than the crude early type, and shows much more variety. The up-to-date spook who has a chance to talk things over with William James, and knows the labyrinths of the human mind is much better adapted to inflict psychal terrors than the illiterate specter of the past. ...

Stories of to-day show a decided advance over the Gothic in the matter of motives for spectral appearance. There are, it is true, certain motives in common between them, but the present-day spirit is less limited, for he has gained the new without loss of the old, if he wishes to keep the old. The principal impulse that impelled classical shades to walk the earth was to request burial, since lacking that he could not enter into the abode of the dead. This appears frequently also in Gothic romance. It is shown but little in recent fiction, perhaps because the modern ghost is reconciled to cremation or is blithely indifferent to what becomes of his body since it no longer rules him. ...Gothic ghosts were also wont to return to show the hiding-place of treasure, but that, too, is dying out as an incentive to haunting. The prosaic explanation here may be that now persons put their treasure in safety deposits, hence there is scant occasion for mystery concerning its location after death. Gothic spooks came back on occasion to reveal parentage, for parents, like valuables, were frequently mislaid in terror romance. This is not so important now, since vital statistics usually keep such matters duly recorded, yet instances do sometimes occur.

Ghosts in the terror romance came to make requests, apart from the petition for burial, which tendency is still observed on the part of later spooks, though not to the same extent as formerly. The requests are psychologically interesting, as they usually relate to simple ties of affection, illustrated by the mother-spirit[6] who asks her friend to take her children. Gothic spirits came back often to make revelations concerning the manner of their death, which is not often the case now, though it does sometimes happen. And Dickens shows us one ghost returning to influence the jury that is trying a man for murder. Specters used to appear to forewarn the living against impending danger, which impulse is rather lacking in later fiction though it still occurs. The curious element of futurity enters into several of these ghostly warnings, as in Dickens's *The Signal Man* where the apparition presages the man's death, as in Algernon Blackwood's story[7] is related the incident of a man who saw the two Indians scalp a white man and drag his body away, at last crying out, "I saw the body, and *the face was my own.*"... This sort of spectral warning, this wireless service for the conveyance of bad news and hint of threatening danger, serves to link the ghost story of the present with those of the past. The records of the Psychical Society show hundreds of such instances, and much use is made in fiction of plots hinging on such motif. ...

The revenge ghost looms large in fiction as in the drama. He was the most important figure in Elizabethan as in classical drama, and Shakespeare's ghosts are principally of that class. ... The revenge ghost is both objective and subjective in his manifestation and his impelling motive adds a touch of frozen horror to his appearance. ... The apparently casual, idle figure that strolls about the docks and streets in *The Detective,* seen by different persons and taken for a man interested only in his own pursuits, is a revenge ghost so relentless that he hounds his victim from country to country, at last killing him by sheer force of terror as he sits on his bed at night, leaving the imprint of his body on the mattress beside the dead man whose face is rigid with mad horror. He has come back in physical embodiment to avenge the betrayal of his daughter. ... The revenge ghost in modern fiction is more varied in forms of manifestation, at times more subtle in suggestion and ghostly psychology, than the conventionalized type of the drama and remains one of the most dreadful of the forms of fear.

[6]In *The Substitute.*
[7]In *A Haunted Island.*

In general, the modern stories show a greater intensity of power in employing the motives that earlier forms had used as well as far greater range of motivation. The earlier ghosts were limited in their impulses, and their psychology was comparatively simple. Not so with the apparitions of to-day. They have a far wider range of motives, are moved by more complex impulses and mixed motivation in many cases difficult to analyze.

The Gothic ghost had some conscience about whom he haunted. He had too much reserve to force himself needlessly upon those that had no connection with his past. If he knew someone that deserved punishment for wrong done him or his, he tried to haunt him and let others alone. The modern ghost is not so considerate. He is actuated in many cases by sheer evil that wreaks itself upon anyone in range. Death gives a terrible immortality and access of power to those whose lives have been particularly evil, and the results are dangerous to society. Dark discarnate hate manifests itself to those within reach. Algernon Blackwood would have us believe that all around us are reservoirs of unspeakable horror and that any moment of weakness on our part may bring down the hosts of damnation upon us. This is illustrated in such stories as *With Intent to Steal,* where the spirit of a man who has hanged himself comes back with hypnotic power forcing others to take their lives in the same way.... If one may judge from ghostly fiction, death subtracts nothing from human emotion but rather adds to it, so that the spectral impulses are more poignant and intense. The darker passions are retained with cumulative power, and there is a terrible immortality of hate, of jealousy and revenge. ...

A comparative study of ghost stories leads one to the conclusion that the ghost is the most modern of ancients and the most ancient of moderns. In some respects the present specter is like and in some unlike the previous forms. Ghosts, whether regarded as conjective or purely subjective, are closely related to the percipients' thoughts. Primitive times produced a primitive supernaturalism and the gradual advance in intellectual development has brought about a heightening and complexity of the weird story. 'Tis in ourselves that ghosts are thus and so!...

The apparitions of to-day have more lines of interest than the ancient ghosts. The Gothic specter was a one-idea creature, with a single-track brain. He was not a ghost-of-all-work as are some of the later spooks. He was a simple-souled being who felt a call to haunt somebody for some purpose or other, so he just went and did it. The specters of to-day are more versatile—they can turn their hand to any kind of haunting that is desired and show an admirable power of adaptability, though there are highly developed specialists as well. The psychology of the primitive ghost and of the Gothic specter was simple. They knew only the elemental passions of love and hate. Gothic spooks haunted the villain or villainess to foil them in their wicked designs or punish them for past misdeeds, or hovered over the hero or heroine to advise, comfort, and chaperon them. But the modern ghosts are not satisfied with such sit-by-the-fire jobs as these. They like to keep in the van of activity and do what mortals do. They run the whole scale of human motions and emotions and one needs as much handy psychology to interpret their hauntings as to read George Meredith. They are actuated by subtle motivations of jealousy, ardent love, tempered friendship, curiosity, mischief, vindictiveness, revenge, hate, gratitude, and all other conceivable impulses. ... The ghost of awful malice, to be explained only on the basis of compound interest of evil stored up for many years, is a new force.

Though the ghostly narrative has shifted its center of gravity from the novel to the short story since Gothic times, and many more of the modern instances are in that form, the supernatural novel has recently taken on a new lease of life. Honors are almost even between the English and the American ghost story, as most of the representative writers on each side turn their pen at some time to write terror tales. The ghost has never lost his power over the human mind. Judging from the past, one may say that the popularity of the ghost story will continue undiminished and will perhaps increase. Certainly there has been a new influx of stories within later times. What mines of horror yet remain untouched for writers of the future, it would be hard to say, yet we do not fear for the exhaustion of the type. On the contrary, ghosts in fiction are becoming so numerous that one wonders if the Malthusian theory will not in time affect them. We are too fond of being fooled by phantoms to surrender them, for "the slow touch of a frozen finger tracing out the spine" is an awesome joy. For ourselves, we are content for the present to function on one plane, but we love to adventure on another plane through spectral substitutes. We may give up the mortal but we'll not willingly give up the ghost.

"Green Tea":
The Archetypal Ghost Story

by Jack Sullivan

In 1839, a new kind of ghost appeared in English fiction. The appearance, in Joseph Sheridan Le Fanu's "Schalken the Painter," went unnoticed, for Le Fanu was an unknown, and his tales were published anonymously. By a strange coincidence, "The Fall of the House of Usher" came out the same year, but Poe's more celebrated tale is a landmark of a different order, an exercise in cosmic paranoia rather than a tale of the supernatural. Le Fanu's creations were real ghosts who stubbornly refused to confine themselves to the shabby psyches of aristocratic neurotics, yet somehow managed to emerge from within as well as invade from without; who (unlike Mrs. Radcliffe's ghosts) could not be explained away, yet who would have nothing to do with what Oliver Onions once called "the groans and clankings of the grosser spook."[1] "Schalken the Painter" was as revolutionary in execution as in the peculiar nature of its two ghosts. The story tells of the abduction, rape, and final seduction of a young woman by a living corpse, all from the point of view of the girl's befuddled uncle and horrified fiancé. Le Fanu handled both the necrophilia and the supernaturalism in the tale with a new anti-Gothic restraint. As if reluctant to reveal its sordid and marvelous secrets, the plot develops itself entirely through suggestion and

"'Green Tea': The Archetypal Ghost Story." From *Elegant Nightmares: The English Ghost Story from Le Fanu to Blackwood* by Jack Sullivan (Athens: Ohio University Press, 1978), pp. 11-31. Copyright © 1978 by Jack Sullivan. Reprinted by permission of the publisher.

[1]Oliver Onions, "Credo," *The Collected Ghost Stories of Oliver Onions* (New York, 1971), p. X.

indirection, building toward an extraordinary dream sequence involving the transformation of a coffin into a Victorian four-poster bed. It is a chilling performance.

Yet "Schalken the Painter" is not the most refined or the most representative of Le Fanu's tales. It is rather the promising start of a long, influential career in ghostly fiction. The culmination of that career is "Green Tea," a late tale which represents the new ghost story in its most uncompromising form. "Green Tea," the story of a man who literally has a monkey on his back, can serve as an ideal introduction not only to Le Fanu's other tales, but to the entire ghostly school that he spawned. It is a thoroughly modern tale, and its modernity, so unexpectedly daring, is the key to understanding the contradictions between plot and theme in more ambivalent tales such as "The Mysterious Lodger" and "The Familiar."

Le Fanu first published "Green Tea" in Dickens's magazine *All the Year Round* (1869) and later reprinted it in *In a Glass Darkly* (1872), a remarkable collection of his late tales which includes "Mr. Justice Harbottle," "The Familiar," "Carmilla," and (somewhat inappropriately since there is no supernatural episode) "The Room in the Dragon Volant." With the possible exception of "Carmilla," no other Le Fanu tale has been so widely discussed. Its visibility, so unusual for Le Fanu, can probably be accounted for by its novel concept. V. S. Pritchett, Edna Kenton, William Buckler, Nelson Browne, and E. F. Benson have all sung the praises of Le Fanu's demonic monkey.[2] Speaking for all of them, Buckler states that "Green Tea" "is generally given first place in the canon of his work," while Pritchett extends the generalization by calling it one of "the best half-dozen ghost stories in the English language."

The structure of "Green Tea" is a perfect illustration of M. R. James's model for the modern ghost story:

[2]V. S. Pritchett, *The Living Novel and Later Appreciations* (New York, 1947), pp. 121-28; Edna Kenton, "A Forgotten Creator of Ghosts," *The Bookman,* 1929, pp. 528-35; *Minor Classics of Nineteenth Century Fiction,* Vol. II, ed. William E. Buckler (Boston, 1967), pp. 27-28; Nelson Browne, *Sheridan Le Fanu* (New York, 1951), pp. 78-80; E. F. Benson, "Sheridan Le Fanu," *The Spectator,* 21 Feb. 1931, p. 264.

> Let us, then, be introduced to the actors in a placid way; let us see them going about their ordinary business, undisturbed by forebodings, pleased with their surroundings; and into this calm environment let the ominous thing put out its head, unobtrusively at first, and then more insistently, until it holds the stage.[3]

Le Fanu was the first to use this strategy, and he applies it with particular deftness here. The victim in "Green Tea," the Reverend Mr. Jennings, is introduced to the reader by the central narrator, Dr. Martin Hesselius, who in the course of the tale becomes Jennings's therapist. We first see Jennings at a congenial, tedious dinner party, conversing with Hesselius. They are discussing a German first edition of Hesselius's "Essays on Metaphysical Medicine." The conversation is learned but also abstracted and rather silly. Only one sentence appears to have any relevance to a possible ghostly experience: it is a hint involving the motivations for Jennings's odd curiosity concerning Hesselius's exotic research: "I suppose [says Hesselius] you have been turning the subject over again in your mind, or something has happened lately to revive your interest in it."[4]

The conversation, with its pedantry and innuendo, is a prefiguration of M. R. James's dialogue, as are the clues which reinforce its implications. Something indeed "has happened." Although Jennings is a reserved, "perfectly gentleman like man," he has a few revealing quirks. For one thing, he has a peculiar tendency to flee from the pulpit during his own sermons: "After proceeding a certain way in the service, he has on a sudden stopped short, and after a silence, apparently quite unable to resume, he has fallen into solitary, inaudible prayer, his hands and eyes uplifted and then pale as death, and in the agitation of a strange shame and horror, descended trembling, and got into the vestry-room, leaving his congregation, without explanation, to themselves" (180). The situation becomes so critical that Jennings resorts to having an alternate clergyman waiting in the wings "should he become thus suddenly incapacitated." Hes-

[3]M. R. James, "Introduction," *Ghosts and Marvels* (London, 1927), p. vi.

[4]*Best Ghost Stories of J. S. Le Fanu*, ed. E. F. Bleiler (New York, 1964), p. 182. Unless otherwise noted, further quotations from Le Fanu's tales will be documented by citing page numbers from the Bleiler edition.

selius also notices a "certain oddity" in Jennings's dinner conversation: "Mr. Jennings has a way of looking sideways upon the
carpet, as if his eye followed the movements of something there"
(180). The final oddity is revealed by the hostess, Lady Mary
Heyduke, when she remarks that she used to quarrel with Jennings over his addiction to green tea. Hesselius agrees that
Jennings was once "extravagantly" addicted to the stuff, but
insists that "he has quite given that up" (183).

Le Fanu, a careful artist, was undoubtedly aware of the ludi-
crousness of all this. The notion that humor is anathema to horror
is one of the persistent clichés of anthology introductions. It is
also one of the most erroneous, as anyone who has read Bierce
or Hartley can attest. Humor, particularly when ironic or absurd,
is inextricably fused with supernatural horror in fiction. I have
found the linkage to be consistent throughout the field: the reader
automatically integrates the two elements as he reads. In "Green
Tea," the first apparition scene skirts the same arbitrary borderline between the laughable and the horrible as the clues which
anticipate it. The absurdity of the premise—the lethal apparition
is, after all, a monkey—weakens the impact not at all; indeed the
strange power of the tale lies in the irony that something intrinsically ridiculous can drive a man to destroy himself.

Jennings, of course, is not amused by this creature. His account of the first apparition is peculiarly unnerving and deserves
to be quoted at length as a paradigm of Le Fanu's apparition
scenes:

> "The interior of the omnibus was nearly dark. I had observed in
> the corner opposite to me at the other side, and at the end next
> the horses, two small circular reflections, as it seemed to me of a
> reddish light. They were about two inches apart, and about the size
> of those small brass buttons that yachting men used to put upon
> their jackets. I began to speculate, as listless men will, upon this
> trifle, as it seemed. From what centre did that faint but deep red
> light come, and from what—glass beads, buttons, toy decorations—
> was it reflected? We were lumbering along gently, having nearly a
> mile still to go. I had not solved the puzzle, and it became in an-
> other minute more odd, for these two luminous points, with a sud-
> den jerk, descended nearer and nearer the floor, keeping still
> their relative distance and horizontal position, and then, as sud-

denly, they rose to the level of the seat on which I was sitting and I saw them no more.

"My curiosity was now really excited and before I had time to think, I saw again these two dull lamps, again together near the floor; again they disappeared, and again in their old corner I saw them.

"So, keeping my eyes upon them, I edged quietly up my own side, towards the end at which I still saw these tiny discs of red.

"There was very little light in the 'bus. It was nearly dark. I leaned forward to aid my endeavour to discover what these little circles really were. They shifted position a little as I did so. I began now to perceive an outline of something black, and I soon saw, with tolerable distinctness, the outline of a small black monkey, pushing its face forward in mimicry to meet mine; those were its eyes, and I now dimly saw its teeth grinning at me.

"I drew back not knowing whether it might not meditate a spring. I fancied that one of the passengers had forgot this ugly pet, and wishing to ascertain something of its temper, though not caring to trust my fingers to it, I poked my umbrella softly towards it. It remained immovable—up to it—*through* it. For through it, and back and forward it passed, without the slightest resistance.

"I can't in the least, convey to you the kind of horror that I felt." (193-194)

Throughout this passage, the emphasis is on the way Jennings perceives the apparition rather than on the apparition itself. Jennings's reaction is the important thing, as is the reader's: we are forced to see this strange abomination exactly as Jennings sees it. It scarcely matters whether the thing is "real" or hallucinated; in a good horror tale this distinction is effaced. Supernatural horror in fiction has little to do with the materiality or immateriality of spooks. What counts is the authenticity of the experience. The scene works because of the intricate perspectival character of the writing, a technique which anticipates Henry James's *The Turn of the Screw* and "Sir Edmund Orme." The most remarkable aspect of Le Fanu's perspectivism is his use of synecdoche, a poetic mechanism which allows him to straddle the boundary between the explicit and the indirect. His use of the device is more radical in other tales, notably "The Haunting of the Tiled House" in which the unearthly force is represented solely by a disembodied hand. Here we visualize the creature in terms of its eyes, although "these two dull lamps" dimly illuminate the rest of the shape.

Jennings stumbles from the omnibus "in a panic" discovering to his "indescribable relief" that the thing is gone. Like all of Le Fanu's victims, he convinces himself that it was all a fleeting "illusion." But on the way home he looks up "with loathing and horror" to see it creeping along beside him on a brick wall. From this point on, the creature persecutes Jennings with incredible tenacity. As in the first apparition scene, the sufferer's emotions are communicated consistently through his reaction to the demon's eyes. During the initial phase of the persecution, the eyes are "dazed and languid," "jaded and sulkey," "sullen and sick." Yet they have "unfathomable malignancy" and above all, "intense vigilance." "In all situations, at all hours," says the unfortunate Jennings, "it is awake and looking at me; that never changes" (196).

Thus begins this extraordinary obsession, chronicled in graded steps: three "stages" in a hellish "journey." In the "Second Stage," the demon mysteriously disappears for a month, during which time Jennings again experiences an illusory respite. But then it returns with "new energy," "brooding over some atrocious plan." This phase of the persecution is characterized by many such disappearances: "it has sometimes been away so long as nearly two months, once for three," Jennings tells his therapist. "Its absence always exceeds a fortnight, although it may be but by a single day. Fifteen days having past since I saw it last, it may return now at any moment" (197). At once arbitrary and mysteriously calculated, this time span induces the maximum amount of anxiety, causing the patient to look progressively "like death." It is a typically cruel touch, which Le Fanu is fond of using in situations of otherworldly harassment (cf. "The Familiar"). Another painful characteristic of the second phase is Jennings's new inability to attain relief by simply shutting his eyes: "I know it is not to be accounted for physically, but I do actually see it though my eyes are closed" (199). As part of its new militancy, the creature will "squat" in Jennings's prayer book during holy services, obscuring any passage he attempts to read his congregation. It is presumably during these occasions that Jennings flees from the pulpit.

In the third and final stage, the demon "speaks" to Jennings. Unlike Gothic writers, with their fatal predilection for chatty spectres, Le Fanu shrewdly avoids any attempt to reproduce its actual words.[5] Instead, he allows Jennings to suggest the sound metaphorically, through a kind of ghostly music: "It is not by my ears it reaches me—it comes like a singing through my head" (200). Although Jennings never quotes the lyrics of this "song," he lets us know that they are thoroughly unpleasant, particularly during his abortive attempts at prayer:

> "This faculty, the power of speaking to me, will be my undoing. It won't let me pray, it interrupts me with dreadful blasphemies. I dare not go on, I could not. Oh! Doctor, can the skill and thought, and prayers of man avail me nothing!" (200)

They indeed avail him nothing. In these tales, prayer is utterly ineffectual—as are faith and good works. Like most Le Fanu, "Green Tea" does not end happily. In the final phase, the demon tries to persuade his victim to commit suicide. Jennings, who after three years of demonic persecution does not need much per-suading, ends his "journey" by cutting his throat. Suicide is the only way out for him, and he is unique among Le Fanu's victims in perceiving this. As in Greek tragedy, the final horror is not rendered directly but is reported by a messenger, in this case Jennings's servant. As always, Le Fanu avoids being too direct: he leaves the awful details to the reader's imagination, yet still gets in a good bloody scene by having Hesselius clinically inspect the "immense pool of blood on the floor" of Jennings's "sombre and now terrible room" (204).

"Green Tea" is every bit as twisted, disturbing and unre-solvable as it seems. Nevertheless, by imposing orthodox ex-planations and theoretical systems on the story, critics have done what they could to dissipate its mystery and menace. The orthodoxies divide into two camps, the Freudian and the Chris-tian, each of which has a predictable explanation for Jennings's persecution. To Peter Penzoldt, Jennings's monkey is simply "the product of schizoid neurosis"; to V. S. Pritchett, it is "dark and hairy with original sin," and its persecutions symbolize "justified"

[5] On the rare occasions when Le Fanu directly quotes a demon's speech, he is careful to include diabolical transformation as a key element in the story. Thus Carmilla speaks, but only in her nonvampiric phases.

retribution for specific sins; to Michael Begnal, the monkey is sent to punish a clergyman who has "lost his faith" and whose "intellectual pride" has "cut him off from God."[6]

The problem with such theories is that they convert possibilities into solutions. M. R. James, who modelled his stories after Le Fanu's, once stated, "It is not amiss sometimes to leave a loophole for a natural explanation, but I would say, let the loophole be so narrow as not to be quite practicable."[7] This teasing, enigmatic quality, so obvious to any writer in the genre, is missed by theory-obsessed critics. In "Green Tea," the Freudian "loophole" is narrow indeed. We are not given enough information about the near-anonymous Jennings to conclude that he is "schizoid" or "sexually repressed." We are told only that he is shy and unassuming.

The Christian interpretation is even flimsier. There is no doubt that Jennings's obsession is somehow connected with an intense, unspeakable feeling of guilt. The text contains many references to this feeling: he collapses from the altar "in the agitation of a strange shame and horror" (180); he looks at Hesselius "guiltily" during their first conversation (182); he even cries "God forgive me!" during a later conversation (192). What the text does not tell us is what Jennings needs to be forgiven for, what crime he has committed to merit such a hideous, ultimately lethal punishment. As we shall see, the only character who could conceivably be accused of "intellectual pride" is Dr. Hesselius. Indeed, if we assume with Begnal that Jennings committed a mortal sin by researching the non-Christian religious beliefs of the ancients, we must ask why Hesselius is not also pursued to the grave by the avenging monkey, for he is guilty of the same heterodox research. Nor is there any evidence that Jennings has lost his faith; on the contrary, he is a pious, devout Christian who ceases to pray only when the monkey literally prevents him from doing so by shrieking blasphemies in his ear.

The truth is that Jennings has done nothing but drink green tea. The very title of the tale registers the fundamental irony: the awful disjuncture between cause and effect, crime and punish-

[6]Peter Penzoldt, *The Supernatural in Fiction* (London, 1952), p. 77; Pritchett, pp. 122-23; Michael H. Begnal, *Joseph Sheridan Le Fanu* (Lewisburg, Pa., 1971), p. 40.

[7]M. R. James, p. vi.

ment. What emerges is an irrational, almost Kafkaesque feeling of guilt and persecution. Like Joseph K., Jennings is ceaselessly pursued and tormented for no discernible reason. A persistent experience in modern fiction is a situation in which the main character wakes up one morning on a tightrope and does not know how he got there. This is precisely the predicament Jennings finds himself in. Although S. M. Ellis calls Le Fanu a "tragic" writer,[8] "Green Tea" is closer to modern tragi-comedy. Jennings never experiences even a flash of tragic recognition; on the contrary, he never knows why this horrible thing is happening. There is no insight, no justice and therefore no tragedy. There is only absurd cruelty, a grim world view which endures in the reader's mind long after the hairs have settled on the back of the neck.

Though ultimately deterministic, this world view is not based on a coherent or knowable determinism—there is neither the benign workings of Providence nor the naturalism of Zola or Dreiser. The sense of doom in these stories emanates from a uniquely hostile cosmos vaguely suggestive of the purblind doomsters which later pursue Thomas Hardy's characters. But Le Fanu is not interested in programmatic philosophical consistency. In trying to get at the source of the horror, various characters suggest various possibilities—all of them bleak—yet final solutions elude them, as they elude the reader. One event leads inexorably to another once the pursuit begins, but the reason behind it is known only to the otherworldly invaders. Causality is present, but Le Fanu's victims experience only Crass Causality, blind and mechanical, yet efficiently murderous once the cosmos gives someone a bad throw of the dice. Jennings dimly perceives the magnitude of the forces massed against him in one of his final, most pathetic speeches:

> "But as food is taken in softly at the lips, and then brought under the teeth, as the tip of the little finger caught in a mill crank will draw in the hand, and the arm, and the whole body, so the miserable mortal who has been once caught firmly by the end of the finest fibre of his nerve, is drawn in and in, by the enormous machinery

---

[8]S. M. Ellis, *Wilkie Collins, Le Fanu and Others* (London, 1931), p. 165. "Tragic" is more applicable to the novels than to the tales. (Ellis finds "a sort of stately inevitableness" in *The House by the Churchyard*.)

> of hell, until he is as I am. Yes, Doctor, as *I* am, for a while I talk
> to you, and implore relief, I feel that my prayer is for the impos-
> sible, and my pleading with the inexorable." (200)

Jennings is horribly right in his perception that the workings of
the grisly machinery are "inexorable" and that his "prayer is for
the impossible."

Despite the resemblance of all this to Hap in its most perverse
manipulations, there is an ominous point at which the analogy
breaks down. Once Le Fanu's hellish machine begins grinding, it
does so with Hardyesque remorselessness, but also with a strange
awareness of purpose which goes beyond the half-consciousness of
the Immanent Will. If Hardy's cosmos is struggling to attain
consciousness, Le Fanu's has already attained it, or is at least well
along the way. If there is no benevolent or rational purpose behind things, there does seem to be a sinister purpose. James
Barton, another Le Fanu victim, speaks of this conspiracy in
Manichaean terms in "The Familiar." Jennings, lacking even
tentative answers, is obsessed with "machinery" and process, with
the "stages" of his torment:

> "In the dark, as you shall presently hear, there are peculiarities.
> It is a small monkey, perfectly black. It had only one peculiarity—
> a character of malignity—unfathomable malignity. During the first
> year it looked sullen and sick. But this character of intense malice
> and vigilance was always underlying that surly languor. During all
> that time it acted as if on a plan of giving me as little trouble as
> was consistent with watching me. Its eyes were never off me. I
> have never lost sight of it, except in my sleep, light or dark, day or
> night, since it came here excepting when it withdraws for some
> weeks at a time, unaccountably.
>
> "In total dark it is visible as in daylight. I do not mean merely its
> eyes. It is *all* visible distinctly in a halo that resembles a glow of red
> embers and which accompanies it in all its movements.
>
> "When it leaves me for a time, it is always at night, in the dark,
> and in the same way. It grows at first uneasy, and then furious, and
> then advances towards me, grinning and shaking, its paws clenched,
> and, at the same time, there comes the appearance of fire in the
> grate. I never have any fire. I can't sleep in the room where there
> is any, and it draws nearer and nearer to the chimney, quivering, it
> seems, with rage, and when its fury rises to the highest pitch, it
> springs into the grate, and up the chimney, and I see it no more.

"When first this happened, I thought I was released. I was now a new man. A day passed—a night—and no return, and a blessed week—a week—another week. I was always on my knees, Dr. Hesselius, always thanking God and praying. A whole month passed of liberty, but on a sudden, it was with me again. ...

"It was with me, and the malice which before was torpid under a sullen exterior, was now active. It was perfectly unchanged in every other respect. This new energy was apparent in its activity and its looks, and soon in other ways.

"For a time, you will understand, the change was shown only in an increased vivacity, and an air of menace, as if it were always brooding over some atrocious plan. Its eyes, as before, were never off me." (196-197)

The victim of "an atrocious plan," intricately conceived and faultlessly executed, Jennings is denied even an inkling of the ultimate purpose behind that plan.

In this sense, Jennings is in a bleaker predicament than Poe's Roderick Usher, who is powerless largely because he thinks he is. Usher's main problem seems to be a kind of self-inflicted catatonia: since the horrors in Poe's tale are completely localized in a single house, they would presumably lessen if Usher would take the narrator's advice and go somewhere else; but the famous twist is that the house cannot be separated from Usher's mind, as Usher himself reveals to us in his allegorical poem and in his abstract paintings of subterranean tunnels.[9] More than anything else, Usher needs a therapist. But Jennings, who has a therapist, is entirely helpless, for the horror which pursues him is more than a psychological phenomenon. Therapy does him no good; he is victimized by something finally independent of his psyche. In the passage describing the monkey's leap up the chimney, Le Fanu is careful to depict a fiend who is extraordinarily alive, the active incarnation of some unrelenting principle of hatred. The symbiotic connection between setting and psyche, so important in "The Fall of the House of Usher" and "MS. Found in a Bottle," does not apply here. Le Fanu's settings are often evocative in themselves (see "Sir Dominick's Bargain"), but they are irrelevant

[9]The most extreme psychoanalytical view of the tale is John S. Hill, "The Dual Hallucination in 'The Fall of the House of Usher,'" *Southwest Review,* XLVIII (1963), 396-402.

to the main action: his doomed heroes are pursued wherever they go, are tormented in the most unlikely places; their ghostly tormenters see no need to confine themselves in depressing Gothic houses and are likely to appear anywhere, often in broad daylight. (In "The Familiar," James Barton is chased by the Watcher, a spectre who is fond of appearing not only in daylight, but in crowds; nor does he mind traveling long distances when Barton tries to skip the country.)

This is not to say that Le Fanu is unconcerned with psychology. On the contrary, his tales deal repeatedly with dark states of consciousness. The difference between "Green Tea" and Edmund Wilson's version of *The Turn of the Screw* is that this inner darkness is a sinisterly accurate measure of the outer world rather than a neurotic projection. Like the madness of Lear, the derangement of Jennings's mind is a mirror image of a derangement in the cosmos, although Jennings has neither the insight nor the catharsis of Lear. That the infernal region in Jennings's psyche reflects not only reality, but the fundamental reality, is hinted at in a passage in Swedenborg's "Arcana Celestia," which Hesselius translated from the Latin:

> "When man's interior sight is opened, which is that of his spirit, then there appear the things of another life, which cannot possibly be made visible to the bodily sight." ...
>
> "By the internal sight it has been granted me to see the things that are in the other life, more clearly than I see those that are in the world. From these considerations, it is evident that external vision exists from interior vision, and this from a vision still more interior, and so on." ...
>
> "If evil spirits could perceive that they were associated with man, and yet that they were spirits separate from him, and if they could flow in into the things of his body, they would attempt by a thousand means to destroy him; for they hate man with a deadly hatred." ...
> (186)

Placing the passage in context with Jennings's experience, it becomes apparent that the doors of perception open straight into hell; they are kept mercifully shut for the most part, but can be flung open by the most absurdly inadvertent act, in this case by the drinking of green tea.

It is just as well that little has been made of Le Fanu's connection with Swedenborg,[10] for Le Fanu's version represents a distortion, or at least a darkening of the original. The passage which Hesselius translates goes on to say that the "wicked genii" do not attack those who are "in the good of faith." The Christian is "continually protected by the lord." But this protection does not work for Jennings (who writes "Deus misereatur mei" in the margin of the Swedenborg text). Without the saving light of a benevolent deity, Le Fanu's mystical psychology is far more malevolent than Swedenborg's: what we have in this psychological landscape are increasingly deeper layers of consciousness, each one increasingly diabolical—an infinite darkness.

The darkness in Le Fanu is quite different from the "blackness of darkness"[11] in Poe or the "great power of blackness" Melville found in Hawthorne.[12] In Poe, darkness is a thick, palpable texture, opaque and impenetrable, which permeates mind and matter like an endless sewage. In Hawthorne, darkness is a moral quality deriving from the traditional symbolic equation of darkness with evil. Both writers paint with a wide brush, darkening their prose immediately with adjectives like "gloomy" and "inscrutable." Though brilliantly evoked, theirs is often a melodramatic world where colors have allegorical rigidity. In Le Fanu, where the fiend is as likely to appear in the full light of the Sunday church service as in the gloom of a mouldering house, where he is comfortable squatting in the prayerbook rather than seething in the sinner's bosom, colors are used sparingly, sometimes monochromatically. Much of the traditional color symbolism remains: the blacks and reds often suggest as much evil and violence as they do in *Macbeth;* the lurid halo emanating from the monkey like "a glow of red embers" gives off the same satanic light as Ethan Brand's lime kiln.

For the most part, however, Le Fanu's colors elude allegorical equations. Unfettered by an orderly moral universe, they have a

---

[10]Neither Ellis nor Browne does any more than mention the connection.

[11] Edgar Allan Poe, "The Pit and the Pendulum," *The Complete Tales and Poems of Edgar Allan Poe* (New York, 1938), p. 246.

[12]Herman Melville, "Hawthorne and His Mosses," reprinted in "Reviews and Letters by Melville," *Moby Dick,* ed Harrison Hayford and Hershel Parker (New York, 1967), p. 540.

half-tinted quality which is somehow more unsettling than the extravagant darkness and storminess of the Gothic writers:

> The sun had already set, and the red reflected light of the western sky illuminated the scene with the peculiar effect with which we are all familiar. The hall seemed very dark, but, getting to the back drawingroom, whose windows command the west, I was again in the same dusky light.
>
> I sat down, looking out upon the richly-wooded landscape that glowed in the grand and melancholy light which was every moment fading. The corners of the room were already dark; all was growing dim, and the gloom was insensibly toning my mind, already prepared for what was sinister. I was waiting alone for his arrival, which soon took place. The door communicating with the front room opened, and the tall figure of Mr. Jennings, faintly seen in the ruddy twilight, came, with quiet stealthy steps, into the room.
>
> We shook hands, and taking a chair to the window, where there was still light enough to enable us to see each other's faces, he sat down beside me, and, placing his hand upon my arm, with scarcely a word of preface began his narrative. . . .
>
> The faint glow of the west, the pomp of the then lonely woods of Richmond, were before us, behind and about us the darkening room, and on the stony face of the sufferer—for the character of his face, though still gentle and sweet, was changed—rested that dim, odd glow which seems to descend and produce, where it touches, lights, sudden though faint, which are lost almost without gradation, in darkness. The silence, too, was utter: not a distant wheel, or bark, or whistle from without; and within the depressing stillness of an invalid bachelor's house. (191)

What do we make of this strange twilight, dim and translucent one minute, "grand and melancholy" the next; "every moment fading," yet reappearing suddenly, only to be "lost, almost without gradation, in darkness"? The passage seems naturalistic enough, at least up to a point (The sunset has "the peculiar effect with which we are all familiar.") Yet the lights and shadows become so blurred and undefined as to become almost interchangeable. Faint points of light seem to go on and off like stars suddenly going out and reappearing in a cloudy sky. In the next to last sentence, with its twisted, almost Jamesian syntax, this "odd glow" is associated with Jennings's face. The "almost" here suggests a subtle gradation, a hierarchy of twilight worlds, each of which gives off its own unearthly lights, swallowing them up again almost instantly.

Jennings has accidentally summoned a creature from one of these worlds, and his face shows the price he has paid: it has assumed the same deathlike appearance as Jennings's new companion; it even emits the same strange lights. Le Fanu's imagery suggests the shifting, dissolving colors of a nightmare. Ambiguous and undefined, his colors are like those in our dreams, much harder to recall than the technicolor images of Poe or Monk Lewis.

The reader can experience the relief of waking, simply by closing the book and turning on every light in the house. The doomed protagonists are not so fortunate. In Jennings's case, his demise seems to be hastened by the incompetence of his therapist. Hesselius deserves close examination, for he appears to be the first psychiatrist in English literature. Since he is pre-Freudian by at least thirty years, he has a hard time defining just what he is, calling himself at various times a medical philosopher, a philosophical physician and even a doctor of Metaphysical Medicine. He is distinctly a therapist, however, claiming to have diagnosed "two hundred and thirty cases more or less nearly akin to that I have entitled 'Green Tea.'" (208). This is a staggering thought, suggesting that Hesselius has dealt with a large number of what are surely the most bizarre patients in the annals of psychiatry. If the prefaces to *In a Glass Darkly* are to be taken seriously, he has had to confront such things as living corpses, demonic monkeys, and lesbian vampires.[18]

All this has been hard on him, as his ineptness in treating Jennings all too clearly reveals. After Jennings unfolds his tale, Hesselius is at an obvious loss as to what to do. At one particularly strained point, immediately following the oration on "the enormous machinery of hell," Hesselius can only say: "I endeavored to calm his visibly increasing agitation and told him that he must

---

[18] With the exception of "Green Tea," none of these confrontations are ever dramatized. Though frequently mentioned in prologues, Hesselius never appears as a character in any of the other tales. Even in "Green Tea," the therapy is interrupted by the patient's suicide before we are able to assess its effectiveness. Unlike Machen's Dr. Raymond, Blackwood's John Silence or Hodgson's Dr. Carnacki (all of whom he anticipates), Hesselius is a background rather than a luminary figure.

not despair" (200). This is fatuous advice: there is every reason
to despair, especially in the absence of any concrete suggestions.
Following Jennings's depressing account of a near-suicide attempt,
Hesselius's advice is even worse:

> "Yes, yes; it is always urging me to crimes, to injure others, or
> myself. You see, Doctor, the situation is urgent, it is indeed. When
> I was in Shropshire, a few weeks, ago" (Mr. Jennings was speaking
> rapidly and trembling now, holding my arm with one hand, and
> looking in my face), "I went out one day with a party of friends
> for a walk: my persecutor, I tell you, was with me at the time. I
> lagged behind the rest: the country near the Dee, you know, is
> beautiful. Our path happened to lie near a coal mine, and at the
> verge of the wood is a perpendicular shaft, they say, a hundred
> and fifty feet deep. My niece had remained behind with me—she
> knows, of course, nothing of the nature of my sufferings. She
> knew, however, that I had been ill, and was low, and she remained
> to prevent my being quite alone. As we loitered slowly on to-
> gether, the brute that accompanied me was urging me to throw
> myself down the shaft. I tell you now—oh, sir, think of it!—the
> one consideration that saved me from that hideous death was the
> fear lest the shock of witnessing the occurrence should be too
> much for the poor girl. I asked her to go on and walk with her
> friends, saying that I could go no further. She made excuses, and
> the more I urged her the firmer she became. She looked doubtful
> and frightened. I suppose there was something in my looks or
> manner that alarmed her; but she would not go, and that literally
> saved me. You had no idea, sir, that a living man could be made so
> abject a slave of Satan," he said with a ghastly groan and a shudder.
>
> There was a pause here, and I said, "You *were* preserved never-
> theless. It was the act of God. You are in his hands, and in the
> power of no other being: be confident therefore for the future."
> (201)

Jennings's concern for the little girl's reaction, even at the climax
of his own suicidal despair, strengthens our feeling that he is a
scrupulously sensitive, compassionate man, undeserving of this
torment. But the passage is more revealing of Hesselius. "You
see, doctor, the situation is urgent, it is indeed" is a chilling
understatement, yet all the philosophic physician can do is offer
platitudes—the solace of a deity who is either indifferent or as
impotent as Hesselius himself. This advice is more than merely

unctuous and ineffectual: the claim that Jennings is "in the power of no other being" is demonstrably false.

Nor does his epilogue, "A Word for Those Who Suffer," do anything to enhance his professional credibility. This final chapter is in the form of a letter to Professor Van Loo of Leyden, a chemist who has suffered from Jennings's malady and whom Hesselius claims to have cured. It is a suspiciously self-serving document:

> Who, under God, cured you? Your humble servant, Martin Hesselius. Let me rather adopt the more emphasized piety of a certain good old French surgeon of three hundred years ago: "I treated, and God cured you."
>
> There is no one affliction of mortality more easily and certainly reducible, with a little patience, and a rational confidence in the physician. With these simple conditions, I look upon the cure as absolutely certain.
>
> You are to remember that I had not even commenced to treat Mr. Jennings' case. I have not any doubt that I should have cured him perfectly in eighteen months, or possibly it might have extended to two years. . . .
>
> You know my tract on "The Cardinal Functions of the Brain." I there, by the evidence of innumerable facts, prove, as I think, the high probability of a circulation arterial and venous in its mechanism, through the nerves. Of this system, thus considered, the brain is the heart. The fluid, which is propagated hence through one class of nerves, returns in an altered state through another, and the nature of that fluid is spiritual, though not immaterial, any more than, as I before remarked, light or electricity are so.
>
> By various abuses, among which the habitual use of such agents as green tea is one, this fluid may be affected as to its quality, but it is more frequently disturbed as to equilibrium. This fluid being that which we have in common with spirits, a congestion found upon the masses of brain or nerve, connected with the interior sense, forms a surface unduly exposed, on which disembodied spirits may operate: communication is thus more or less effectually established. Between this brain circulation and the heart circulation there is an intimate sympathy. The seat, or rather the instrument of exterior vision, is the eye. The seat of interior vision is the nervous tissue and brain, immediately about and above the eyebrow. You remember how effectually I dissipated your pictures by the simple application of iced eau-de-cologne. Few cases, however,

can be treated exactly alike with anything like rapid success. Cold
acts powerfully as a repellant of the nervous fluid. Long enough
continued it will even produce that permanent insensibility which
we call numbness, and a little longer muscular as well as sensational
paralysis.

I have not, I repeat, the slightest doubt that I should have first
dimmed and ultimately sealed that inner eye which Mr. Jennings
had inadvertently opened. ... It is by acting steadily upon the
body, by a simple process, that this result is produced—and inevitably produced—I have never yet failed.

Poor Mr. Jennings made away with himself. But that catastrophe
was the result of a totally different malady, which, as it were, projected itself upon the disease which was established. His case was
in the distinctive manner a complication, and the complaint under
which he really succumbed, was hereditary suicidal mania. Poor
Mr. Jennings I cannot call a patient of mine, for I had not even
begun to treat his case, and he had not yet given me, I am convinced, his full and unreserved confidence. If the patient do not
array himself on the side of the disease, his cure is certain. (206-207)

The immediate point of interest here is the earnest but tortured
attempt to reconcile medical science with mystical experience, a
commonplace exercise in nineteenth and early twentieth-century weird fiction.[14] In relation to the story, however, the epilogue
is not so earnest. It raises a variety of questions. Why did Hesselius
not share any of these insights with his patient, a man on the
verge of self-destruction? Why did he not tell him that his cure
would be a "simple process"? Why did he not describe this process
and thereby relieve Jennings's paranoia? Leaving aside the be-
lievability of this "absolutely certain" cure why did he not produce the magical "iced eau-de-cologne" and douse the wretched
man with it? The final dismissal of Jennings's case as "hereditary
suicidal mania," without any evidence, is an ugly rationaliza-
tion. The wonder is that Jennings, unremittingly persecuted for
three years, did not kill himself sooner; if anything, the evidence
indicates an unusually strong psyche.

[14] Of all the writers who attempted this fusion—Stevenson, Bulwer-Lytton,
Machen, Blackwood, Hodgson, and Wells (among others)—only Wells seems to
have recognized that the polarities must be reconciled with the aesthetic demands of the story as well as with each other. Compare Wells's "The Plattner
Story" with Bulwer-Lytton's "The House and the Brain": one is an integrated
work of fiction, the other a story interrupted (and subverted) by an essay.

But the oddest thing about this addendum is its failure to explain its author's behaviour in the period between Jennings's narration and his suicide. After giving his account, Jennings understandably breaks down weeping (despite Hesselius's disingenuous "He seemed comforted"). Hesselius does have one concrete bit of comfort to offer: "One promise I exacted, which was that should the monkey return, I should be sent for immediately" (202). Taking his doctor at his word, Jennings tries to contact Hesselius "immediately" after the monkey's next appearance, which is predictably soon:

> Dear Dr. Hesselius—It is here. You had not been an hour gone when it returned. It is speaking. It knows all that has happened. It knows everything—it knows you, and is frantic and atrocious. It reviles. I send you this. It knows every word I have written—I write. This I promised and I therefore write, but I fear very confused, very incoherently, I am so interrupted, disturbed. (203)

Hesselius, however, is not to be found. Intentionally making his whereabouts unknown, he has fled when he is most needed to an unknown address where he intends to dabble with his metaphysical medicines "without the possibility of intrusion or distraction" (202). He seems to need therapy himself, so shut off is he from the consequences of his actions. The immediate consequence is that Jennings, feeling totally alone, cuts his throat.

Hesselius is only marginally concerned with the well-being of his patient. His chief motivation—which reaches a state of frenzied anticipation—is his determination to validate his theories. As the epilogue implies, he is less saddened than annoyed by his patient's death; by that act, Jennings has robbed him of his big chance.

We can reasonably conclude that Le Fanu did not mean us to take this epilogue on the same level of seriousness as Hesselius assumes we do. His claims, accusations, and actions are dubious enough in themselves; set against the powerful authenticity of Jennings's narrative, they make sense only as dramatic irony. Unless seen as ironic, the "Word for Those Who Suffer" becomes an aesthetic blunder. There is nothing organic about this final chapter; it seems distinctly tacked on, a needless diatribe which ruins the tale if taken at face value. But seen as ironic, it underscores the hopelessness of Jennings's predicament.

As the less than reliable narrator of a horror tale, Hesselius is part of a tradition which begins with Poe's narrator in "The Tell-Tale Heart" and culminates in the governess's account in *The Turn of the Screw.* This is not to say that Hesselius is a Gothic villain—a frothing madman or an ostentatiously evil doctor. Like everything else in the story, he is difficult to pin down: earnest and well-meaning in the opening pages, he seems progressively more ineffectual, even senile, at worst evincing a precarious ego which distorts his judgment. In other respects as well, the narrative problems are more complex than those in Poe. Hesselius is not the only narrator of "Green Tea." The tale has a prologue as well as a conclusion; as William Buckler has shown, the prologue is also problematic:

> The story is filtered to the reader through three "carefully educated" men of science: the supposed editor, or "medical secretary"; Dr. Hesselius, the narrator; and Professor Van Loo, chemist and student of history, metaphysics, and medicine, to whom a correspondent would presumably write with conscientiousness. And yet each is a fallible authority: the editor is a confessed "enthusiast" who has taken Dr. Hesselius as his "master"; Dr. Hesselius, besides suffering from an acutely sensitive ego, obviously has no authority within the medical fraternity, is theoretical and categorical, and seems unduly intent upon rationalizing the perfect record of his "cures," and Dr. Van Loo, according to the narrator, has suffered from a similar "affection," while, according to the editor, he is an "unlearned reader."[15]

Though accurate and concise as a summary, Buckler's introduction does not attempt to resolve the obvious question it raises: why does Le Fanu bother with this narrative filtering device at all? This is a difficult question to answer, for "Green Tea" is unlike other tales which saddle us with unreliable or multiple narrators: we get little sense of the moral complexity found in Stevenson, the pathological involutions found in Poe, or the fanatically refined sensibility found in Henry James.

As an intentionally fuzzy narrative, "Green Tea" is similar to several tales in Ambrose Bierce's *In the Midst of Life* and *Can*

[15]Buckler, p. 27.

Such Things Be? Like Bierce's "The Moonlit Road" and "The Suitable Surroundings," "Green Tea" seems arbitrarily burdened with narrators and editors.[16] Yet the seeming arbitrariness of the narrative scheme imparts a unique atmosphere to these tales. Le Fanu anticipates Bierce in his evocation of a world where things refuse to fit together, where terrible things happen to the wrong people for the wrong reasons, where horrors leap out of the most trivial or ridiculous contexts. The disjointedness of the narrative pattern reinforces our sense of a nightmare world where everything is out of joint. Why should we expect aesthetic order when monkeys can chase people into their graves, green tea can cause damnation, and therapists can suddenly drop out of sight when patients are on the precipice of suicide? Besides instilling a sense of underlying chaos, the filtering device also gives the impression of narrative distance, a useful effect in any kind of ironic fiction, but particularly necessary in the ghost story, where too much narrative directness can instantly blunt the desired impact. Jennings must seem like a thoroughly helpless creature, dwarfed by diabolical forces beyond his comprehension (let alone control) and gradually receding from our vision into hell. What could serve this purpose better than to have his narrative manipulated by three verbose doctors who are more concerned with selling their theories than with protecting his sanity?

Le Fanu's complicated narrative skein also helps create the "loophole" of ambiguity mentioned by M. R. James. It is at least *possible* that Hesselius's claims are justified, that his unorthodox medications would have banished Jennings's monkey, and that his infallibility is "absolutely certain." (Although this certainty would not efface the supernatural element in the story, it would have the disappointing effect of a natural explanation: demonic forces might still exist in some sense, but would be so easily subdued by infallible German doctors as to be in effect naturalized.) For the many reasons mentioned, however, we doubt Hesselius's word: the easy way out is a remote possibility but "not quite practicable." Even if Hesselius were believable as

---

[16]Although brief, "The Moonlit Road" achieves an almost mind-numbing complexity by emerging from three fragmented points of view, including that of the murder victim as communicated through a medium. "The Suitable Surroundings" juxtaposes time sequences as well as narrators, in each case creating a maximum of confusion which gives the tale a peculiarly delayed impact.

the medical equivalent of a Dickensian benefactor (dispensing cures instead of money at the end), we would still be left with the terrible irony of Jennings destroying himself just as he is about to be delivered.

Either way, "Green Tea" is a horror tale. It is Le Fanu's most extreme, yet most controlled performance. Although the "well managed crescendo" admired by M. R. James occurs in most of his tales, nowhere is it more attenuated and cumulative than in "Green Tea." In "Schalken the Painter," "Chief Justice Harbottle" and others, the initial apparition comes fairly quickly; here the "journey" is more leisurely and spread out; the distance travelled is greater. By taking his time, Le Fanu makes Jennings's "doors of perception" experience all the more painful and catastrophic. Similarly, the heavy use of ambiguity and dramatic irony suggests a dislocated, strangely modern world where reality is grim enough to outpace our most exaggerated fantasies. Though written in the late nineteenth century, "Green Tea," as E. F. Benson has happily put it, is "instinct with an awfulness which custom cannot stale."[17] Those who find ghost stories boring or silly will probably interpret "awfulness" in a different way than Benson intended. But the rest of us know exactly what he means.

[17]Benson, pp. 263-64.

Dracula: The Gnostic Quest
and Victorian Wasteland

by Mark M. Hennelly, Jr.

In *Dracula* (1897), when Mina Harker reads her husband's Transylvanian journal and relates it to the recent enigmatic events in London, she discovers that "There seems to be through it all some thread of continuity"[1]; and the attentive reader makes an identical discovery in Bram Stoker's long-neglected tale of two cultures. Until now there have been occasional folkloric,[2] psycho-sexual,[3] and even political[4] readings of the novel; but such studies generally see this horror classic as a *sui generis* phenomenon and not as a sign of the times, not as a drama of conflicting epistemologies, which is so much a part of the Victorian tradition and which Dracula presents with brutal candor. Although the "Gothic" tradition is peripheral to this study, it is even more surprising that treatments of the Gothic or Romantic

"Dracula: The Gnostic Quest and Victorian Wasteland" by Mark M. Hennelly, Jr. From *English Literature in Transition: 1880-1920,* Vol. 20, No. 1, 1977, pp. 13-25. Copyright by H. E. Gerber and H. S. Gerber on behalf of the author. Some footnotes have been shortened. Reprinted by permission of the publisher and the author.

[1]Bram Stoker, *Dracula* (N.Y.: Modern Library, 1897), p. 96. All subsequent quotations are from this edition and are incorporated within the text.

[2]See Grigore Nandris, "The Historical Dracula: The Theme of His Legend in the Western and in the Eastern Literatures of Europe," *Comparative Literature Studies,* III: 4 (1966), 367-96.

[3]See C. F. Bentley, "The Monster in the Bedroom: Sexual Symbolism in Bram Stoker's *Dracula,"* *Literature and Psychology,* XXII:1 (1972), 27-34; and Joseph S. Bierman, "Dracula: Prolonged Childhood Illness, and the Oral Triad," *American Imago,* XXIX (Summer 1972), 186-98.

[4]See Richard Wasson, "The Politics of *Dracula,"* *English Literature in Transition,* IX:1 (1966), 24-27.

novel have almost totally neglected Stoker's most terrifying example of the genre. For instance, in Robert Kiely's otherwise excellent *The Romantic Novel in England,* the generic definition seems written precisely for *Dracula:* "the most daring thematic innovations of the romantic novelists—the use of the supernatural and of wild nature, of dreams and madness, of physical violence and perverse sexuality—are played ironically or melodramatically against the conventions which they impugn. In terms of setting, tone, and character grouping, romantic novelists often seem to be writing two books in one." However, on the next and final page, he concludes: "After *Wuthering Heights,* it is difficult to find any work which carries the possibilities of intuition, subjectivity, or lyricism further in the novel without losing the old fashioned outlines of form altogether."[5]

It is the thesis of this study that besides being a masterpiece of Gothicism (which itself is ultimately concerned with the problem of *belief* in the Demiurge), *Dracula* is an allegory of rival epistemologies in quest of a gnosis which will rehabilitate the Victorian wasteland; and as its conclusion dramatizes, this rehabilitation demands a *transfusion,* the metaphor is inevitable, from the blood-knowledge of Dracula. Caught between two worlds, the now anemic nineteenth century all but dead, the twentieth powerless to be born without fertile, ideological conception, fin-de-siècle England desperately needs redemption. As Van Helsing announces: "we go out as the old knights of the Cross to redeem. ...we are pledged to set the world free" (pp. 354-55).

Symbolizing the battleground between Ancients and Moderns, the Wasteland often provides a psychoscape for Victorian poetry and fiction: and the "waste land" of Tennyson's "Morte d'Arthur," the "ominous tract" of Browning's "Childe Roland," Arnold's "darkling plain" of "Dover Beach," Dickens' Coketown, and Hardy's Egdon Heath are just some examples of its prevalent imagery. In fact, in his study of the subject, Curtis Dahl concludes: "The wasteland, often thought to be a modern discovery, had been thoroughly explored by the Victorians before the twentieth century was born."[6] In *Dracula,* Dr. Seward, alter-ego for the Vic-

[5](Cambridge, Mass.: Harvard University Press, 1972), pp. 254-55.

[6]"The Victorian Wasteland," in *Victorian Literature: Modern Essays in Criticism,* ed. by Austin Wright (London, Oxford, N.Y.: Oxford University Press, 1961), p. 40.

torian reader, makes clear the relationship between his wasted London, "under brown fog" like T. S. Eliot's, and his own blasted, scientific beliefs: "It was a shock for me to turn from the wonderful smoky beauty of a sunset over London, with its lurid lights and inky shadows and all the marvellous tints that come on foul clouds even as on foul water, and to realize all the grim sternness of my own cold stone building, with its wealth of breathing misery, and my own desolate heart to endure it all" (pp. 127-28). Here the oxymoron suggests that even naturally-wasted London is better than his own artifically-petrified, "desolate heart." However, the most salient passage for the wasteland theme, and one of the more remarkable passages in Victorian literature, locates the "waste of desolation" (p. 418) in London's geographic other-self, Transylvania—even the repeated *desolate* condition serves to link the two cultures. The broken-English here is characteristically Van Helsing's; and this description of Dracula's motivation and kingdom prompts his already mentioned pledge to "set the world free":

> I have told them how the measure of leaving his own barren land—barren of peoples—and coming to a new land where life of man teems till they are like the multitude of standing corn, was the work of centuries. Were another of the Un-Dead, like him, to try to do what he has done, perhaps not all the centuries of the world that have been, or that will be, could aid him. With this one, all the forces of nature that are occult and deep and strong must have worked together in some wondrous way. The very place, where he have been alive, Un-Dead for all these centuries, is full of strangeness of the geologic and chemical world. There are deep caverns and fissures that reach none know whither. There have been volcanoes, some of whose openings still send out waters of strange properties and gases that kill or make to vivify. Doubtless, there is something magnetic or electric in some of these combinations or occult forces which work for physical life in strange way; and in himself were from the first some great qualities. In a hard and warlike time he was celebrate that he have more iron nerve, more subtle brain, more braver heart, than any man. In him some vital principle have in strange way found their utmost; and as his body keep strong and grow and thrive, so his brain grow too. All this without that diabolic aid which is surely to him; for it have to yield to the powers that come from, and are, symbolic of good (p. 353).

The meaning of this lengthy passage is central to the understanding of *Dracula*. Both nocturnal-lunar Translyvania and
diurnal-solar London[7] are "barren land[s] "; and each desperately
needs the strength of the other to heal its own sterility. In this
sense, not only do the Occidental vampire hunters embark upon a
"great quest" (p. 259), "a wild adventure...into unknown places
and unknown ways" (p. 395); but Dracula similarly initiates "his
quest" (p. 48) for an unknown gnosis. Dracula with his ancient
"child-brain" searches for the "man-brain" (pp. 376-77) of modern
self-consciousness; while what Van Helsing calls the "man-brains"
of the Londoners seek the primitive passion and natural energy of
the non-repressed "child-brain" *(ibid.)* of Transylvania, a condition the British recall subliminally in both memory and desire.
In this sense the novel's action concerns the intimate relationships between the two corollary quests and between past and present values. Moreover, the above excerpt reveals that Dracula is a
kind of primitive Corn God who "directs the elements" (p. 263),
a Fisher King (Stoker's dream of a "vampire king rising from his
tomb" precipitated the novel)[8] who has anachronistically as "this
man-that-was" (p. 264) lived long past his prime and rests in an
unholy Perilous Chapel (p. 265). Now he must be slain and replaced by a viable, young, twentieth-century totem—at least he
must be slain and his energy reabsorbed if the London wasteland
is to be renewed and if Eliot's "hooded hordes swarming" are to
be checked. Thus, although once a "vital principle...symbolic
of good," the Count's energy is now only malign. At the cosmic
level of the "geologic and chemical world," Dracula's *élan vital,*
these "gases," can either "kill or make to vivify" depending, at the

[7]See p. 128 for a discussion of the "malign influence" of sun and moon at different periods, and p. 264 for a discussion of the limitations of the Count's lunar
powers. This "dual life" theme has, of course, become a touchstone for criticism
of nineteenth-century literature. For example, John E. Stoll remarks: "Inherited
in great part from the 18th century separation of intellect and feeling, judgement
and fancy, sense and sensibility, psychological duality is a distinctive characteristic of the 19th century as a whole, affects all forms of literature, and should not
be confined to the American *or* British novel alone" in "Psychological Dissocia-
tion in the Victorian Novel," *Literature and Psychology,* XX:2 (1970), 63-64. See
also Masao Miyoshi's book-length treatment of the subject, *The Divided Self*
(N.Y. New York University Press, 1969).

[8]See H. Ludlam, *A Biography of Dracula: The Life Story of Bram Stoker*
(London: W. Foulsham, 1962), pp. 99-100.

personal level, on whether they are repressed as with Lucy, or honestly accepted as with Mina.

However, we anticipate ourselves. Let us simply conclude by hearing two clarifying but general appraisals of cultural repression, neither of which has *Dracula* in mind. First, Carl Jung describes fiction dealing with the "collective unconscious" in a way particularly relevant to "all the forces of nature that are occult and deep and strong": It "is a strange something that derives its existence from the hinterland of man's mind—that suggests the abyss of time separating us from the pre-human ages, or evokes a super-human world of contrasting light and darkness. It is a primordial experience which surpasses man's understanding, and to which he is in danger of succumbing. The value and the force of the experience are given by its enormity. It arises from timeless depths; it is foreign and cold, many-sided, demonic and grotesque."[9] Secondly, Elliot Gose ends his discussion of the nineteenth-century "Irrational" novel (again, *Dracula* is omitted) with an evaluation peculiarly suited to Stoker's archetypal drama and anticipating the symbolism of Dracula's "orderly disorder" (p. 331) in London: "Beneath the ordered society of his time each [novelist of the Irrational] saw an unordered chaos, a world disintegrating, a new order waiting to be established. Each saw a spectacle, perhaps because it was true of Victorian society, but more fundamentally because each had descended within himself and confronted in that heart of darkness not only the death of life, but the unborn shape of future life. Their novels embody that life."[10]

As stated earlier, the quest to redeem this wasteland is not a search for a literal grail or treasure, but as Van Helsing understands a search for redemptive knowledge: "We shall go to make our search—if I can call it so, for it is not a search but knowing" (p. 348). Many literary historians have found this gnostic quest to be the central theme of nineteenth-century letters and of the Victorian arts in particular. Morse Peckham, for example, labels the endeavor the "orientative drive" and devotes his entire

[9]*Modern Man in Search of a Soul* (London: Routledge & Kegan Paul, 1933), pp. 180-81.

[10]*Imagination Indulged: The Irrational in the Nineteenth-Century Novel* (Montreal and London: McGill-Queen's University Press, 1972), p. 176. Gose also cites the above quotation from Jung, pp. 173-74.

Beyond the Tragic Vision[11] to pursuing the many varieties of this quest. Kristian Smidt, on the other hand, limiting his treatment to "The Intellectual Quest of the Victorian Poets," discovers that "Characteristically the poetry of the Victorian period deals with a search or quest—for knowledge or for something symbolizing knowledge and certainty."[12] And a novel like *Silas Marner,* with its repeated insistence on traditional *faith, belief,* and *trust* in the face of the *mysteries* of life, perfectly exemplifies the orthodox Victorian solution. Thus once-doubting Silas finally discovers the continuity between past and present epistemologies and thereby renews his personal wasteland: "By seeking what was needful for Eppie, by sharing the effect that everything produced on her, he had himself come to appropriate the forms of custom and belief which were the mould of Raveloe life; and as, with reawakening sensibilities, memory also reawakened, he had begun to ponder over the elements of his old faith, and blend them with his new impressions, till he recovered a consciousness of unity between past and present" (Chapt. 16).

Dracula, however, explores the unorthodox and alien beliefs demanded by Van Helsing's hypothesis that "There are always mysteries in life" (p. 210). As he repeatedly insists to Seward and the others: "I want you to believe....To believe in things you cannot. Let me illustrate. I heard once of an American who so defined faith: 'that faculty which enables us to believe things we know to be untrue.' For one, I follow that man. He meant that we shall have an open mind..." (p. 211). The action of the novel dramatizes the gnostic value of this "open mind" and concurrently tests the epistemological flexibility of various frames of mind: Scepticism (pp. 260, 367-68), Transcendentalism (p. 373), Empiricism and the Philosophy of Crime (p. 377), Superstition (pp. 262-63), and most importantly, Scientific-Rationalism: "our scientific, sceptical, matter-of-fact nineteenth-century" (p. 262). As Van

[11](N.Y.: George Braziller, 1962), *passim.*

[12]In *British Victorian Literature: Recent Revaluations,* ed. by Shiv Kumar (N.Y.: New York University Press, 1969), pp. 54-55. ...For other relevant discussions of the gnostic quest in nineteenth-century literature, see L. J. Swingle, "Frankenstein's Monster and Its Romantic Relatives: Problems of Knowledge in English Literature," *Texas Studies in Literature and Language,* XV (Spring 1973), 51-66, and my "Oedipus and Orpheus in the Maelstrom: The Traumatic Rebirth of the Artist," *Poe Studies,* IX (June 1976), pp. 6-11.

Helsing iconoclastically charges: "Ah, it is the fault of our science that it wants to explain all; and if it explains not, then it says there is nothing to explain" (p. 209). And again: "in this enlightened age, when men believe not even what they see, the doubting of wise men would be his [Dracula's] greatest strength" (p. 355). Consequently, the quest for the Count is actually a quest for the all-believing "open-mind" which, like Silas Marner's, can accommodate both past superstitions and present faith, for as Van Helsing believes: "to superstition we must trust at first; it was man's faith in the early, and it have its root in faith still" (p. 362). And it is past superstitions, particularly the belief in vampires and Dracula's blood-knowledge, from which English orthodox faith so desperately needs a transfusion. As Walter E. Houghton indicates in *The Victorian Frame of Mind*—and this paradox is what makes *Dracula* a tell-tale sign of the times—"The Victorian mind was rigid and dogmatic, but it was criticized [for being so]." However: "It looks as if the open and flexible mind was also Victorian because, unlike the rigid-dogmatic mind with its long history, it was largely indigenous to the nineteenth century."[13]

From the novel's brief Preface (omitted in some editions) to its postscript Note, the epistolary style also argues for the gnostic condition of the "open mind." The Preface maintains that such a collection of personal and public papers "given from the standpoint and within the range of knowledge of those who made them" insures "that a history almost at variance with the possibilities of later-day belief may stand forth as simple fact" (p. vii). Again, the emphasis here revolves around the questions of "range of knowledge," "later-day belief," and "simple fact," inherent in earlier-day superstitions, that vampires do exist. Moreover, the epistolary style always insists upon the relativity of knowledge and the problems of absolute certainty. And here, although Stoker "borrowed" his style from contemporary Wilkie Collins,[14] it nevertheless, observing Kiely's criterion of maintaining "old fashioned outlines of form," thematically links Samuel Richardson and the past dawn of English fiction with present practice. Lionel Stevenson's remarks on "The Relativity of Truth in Victorian Fiction" are consequently relevant here: "They [Victorian novelists] stand

[13](New Haven and London: Yale University Press, 1957), p. 176.
[14]See Ludlam, p. 101.

as transitional figures between the confidence in objective fact
that characterizes the age of reason and the unabashed solipsism
that came into fiction in the present century through the stream
of consciousness technique."[15] In another sense, the disappear-
ance of an omniscient narrator in *Dracula* reflects the atrophy of
God and traditional faith so symptomatic of the Victorian wasteland; hence the small, central group of splintered selves is also
searching for a new stockpile of communal and personal values.
As J. Hillis Miller states the problem: "If Victorian fiction
focuses on inter-human relations as the arena of a search for self-
fulfillment, this search is governed not only by the apparent
absence of God but also by the effacement of any ontological
foundation for the self."[16] The last words of the postscript Note
echo the diction of the Preface as Harker reports Van Helsing's
final thoughts on gnostic credibility: "We want no proofs; we ask
none to believe us! This boy [Harker's son] will someday know.
...later on he will understand..." (p. 418). Thus, and as we shall
later see, it is this final symbol of the new, twentieth-century man
who will ultimately inherit the renewed wasteland and this collective testimonial and legacy of open-minded belief, the novel itself.

By dramatizing the intimate identity between Transylvania
and London, between vampirism and civilization, the circular
structure of *Dracula,* whose locale shifts from the Carpathians to
England and then back to Transylvania, also reveals the thematic
link between the epistemologies of the two wasted kingdoms. The
central point, as Van Helsing understands, is: "For it is not the
least of its terrors that this evil thing is rooted deep in all good"
(p. 265). Or in the cockney accents of Thomas Bilder, the London
zoo-keeper: "there's a deal of the same nature in us as in them
theer animiles" (p. 149). For example, Dracula's castle is a schizoid ˙
dwelling with upper, fashionable apartments and even a Victorian library but also with lower crypts and vaults; while, analog-
ously, Dr. Seward's Victorian mansion conceals a lunatic asylum,
complete with fledgling vampire, beneath it. Dracula has three
lovers; Lucy has three suitors. Dracula hypnotizes; Van Helsing
hypnotizes. Dracula sucks blood; Van Helsing transfuses blood;

[15]In *Victorian Essays: A Symposium,* ed. by Warren D. Anderson and Thomas
D. Clareson (Oberlin, Ohio: Kent State University Press, 1967), p. 86.
   [16]*The Form of Victorian Fiction* (Notre Dame and London: University of
Notre Dame Press, 1968), p. 45.

and once, in fact, Seward "suck[ed] " (p. 124) blood from a gan-grenous wound of Van Helsing. Dracula wears Harker's British clothes to steal babies and later in London even wears a "hat of straw" (p. 350). Additionally, there is a consistently-stressed analogy between vampirism and christianity; and both, given the insights of Frazer, Jessie Weston and Freud's *Totem and Taboo,* seem related to the Oedipal Fisher-King and the wasteland. Thus vampirism deals with "zoophagy"; christianity with eating the body and drinking the blood of Christ—"the Scriptural phrase, 'For the blood is the life!'" (p. 257). Both employ numerous rituals and complicated liturgy, for example "the Vampire's baptism of blood" (p. 356). And lastly, both are locked in a theomachy for control of the world (Crucifix and Host against Demiurge), as Van Helsing notes: "the devil may work against us for all he's worth, but God sends us men when we want them" (p. 163). In fact, as Robert Stevens argues in "The Exorcism of England's Gothic Demon," the Irish sensibility (like Stoker's) is more aware of such epistemological problems with religious "certainty": "If that faith in things seen, that affirmative belief that the cosmos 'functions,' can be interpreted as a British and protestant faith, then one should not be surprised to find a more intense collective anxiety manifest in Catholic Ireland."[17] At any rate, the holistic and redemptive knowledge which understands this primal identity between "the world...of good men [and] ...monsters" (p. 246) enables the Victorians to use "various armaments—the spiritual in the left hand, the mortal in the right" (p. 336). Finally, it teaches, in the words of Van Helsing's favorite meta-phor, that the *felix culpa,* or fortunate fall to belief in vampires, is the only way to save the wasteland: we "must pass through the bitter waters to reach the sweet" (p. 222, see also pp. 133, 187). Or as Harker learns, each "new pain" is a "means to a good end" (p. 363).

Turning to the allegorical characters, we discover the same Victorian concern with wasteland sterility, open-minded episte-mology, and Jekyll-Hyde repression. Renfield, first of all, is a native zoophagist or vampire, one alive and unwell in London before the "foreign" Dracula is ever smuggled ashore. Thus his manic-depressive schizophrenia, that "combination" of "homo-

[17]*Midwest Quarterly,* XIV (Winter 1973), 152.

cidal and religious mania" (p. 111), is emblematic of the latent
dualism in the Victorian personality; and his lunacy must be
made manifest and resolved for the solar wasteland to be renewed.
If so unveiled and openly tamed or domesticated, Renfield's
manic but vital energy can certainly prove therapeutic and reveal
the inner "method in his madness" (p. 76). He then may truly and
wholly become the visionary epistemologist "talking elemental
philosophy...with the manner of a polished gentleman" (p. 257).
And the rich potential of this new, gentle man, not bound by the
rigidity of caste like Lord Godalming, is most apparent when
Renfield self-sacrificially uses his vampire-madness to attempt
to trap the Count and save Mina (pp. 360 ff.). Consequently, and
much like Harker, Renfield's wish "not to deceive myself" allows
him to distinguish between "dream" and "grim reality" (p. 306)
and makes this "sanest lunatic" (p. 273) an epistemological model
for the other Victorians. As Van Helsing admits: "I may gain
more knowledge out of the folly of this madman than I shall from
the teaching of the most wise" (p. 281).

Quincey Morris, the Texan and prior suitor of Lucy, is not quite
as simple-minded as he seems; or at least his simple-mindedness
finally becomes an analogue of open-mindedness. Like Van Helsing and Dracula, he represents a foreign quality which the Victorians need to absorb. Because of his preoccupation with knives
and Winchesters, it is easy enough to see Morris, the "dominant
spirit" (p. 337), as the symbol of potent, non-paralyzed activity,
"always...the one to arrange the plan of action" *(ibid.)*. However,
the fact that "Quincey's head is level" (p. 294), that "His head is
what you call in plane with the horizon" (p. 324), and most importantly that he "accepts all things, and accepts them in the spirit
of cool bravery" (p. 230), all suggest that he suffers neither from
wasteland duality nor gnostic rigidity. Hence it is most fitting
that the new man, the Harkers' child, should be called primarily
Quincey, besides, as we will see, his other tacit names.

Arthur Holmwood, or *Lord* Godalming, emblemizes class,
wealth, and aristocratic values, all instances of decay in the Victorian wasteland. As Renfield, the potential true gentleman,
characterizes the gentleman cult: "you...who by nationality, by
heredity,...are fitted to hold your respective" place in society
(p. 268). Discussing this epistemological "Problem of Spiritual

Authority in the Nineteenth Century," Northrop Frye relevantly observes that "The ascendant class, therefore, and more particularly the aristocracy, comes to represent an ideal authority, expressed in the term 'gentleman,' at the point in history at which its effective temporal authority has begun to decline.... The special function of the aristocracy has always included the art of putting on a show, of dramatizing a way of life."[18] However, like King Arthur, this Arthur's way of life is finally ineffectual; his aristocratic code is too divorced from natural values as symbolized by his replacement of the natural *Holmwood* with the divine-right *(God-)* of noblesse oblige pedigree *(-alming)*. Thus his bride-to-be is appropriately seduced by Dracula, the demiurge of the natural world; and Arthur's sterile lack of open-minded belief renders him unable "to believe things we know to be untrue." As he confesses to Van Helsing: "I did not trust you because I did not know you" (p. 243). Consequently, chivalric Arthur "make[s] the only atonement in my power" (p. 243) which, actually, is the provision of funds and influences for the vampire hunt. Thus he loses his Guinevere and wastes his kingdom.

Dr. Seward represents Science but is also the detached alter-ego of the skeptical Victorian reader since his diary consumes so much of the narrative and since what he calls "the dogged argumentativeness of my nature" (p. 217) provokes him repeatedly to question belief in the unknown: "Surely there must be *some* rational explanation of all these mysterious things" (p. 223, italics Stoker's). Thus Van Helsing instructs Seward along with the reader, clue by clue, about the existence of vampires. As the good doctor remarks: "Professor, let me be your pet student again. Tell me the thesis, so that I may apply your knowledge as you go on. At present I am going in my mind from point to point as a mad man, and not a sane one, follows an idea" (p. 211). Moreover, and as this temporary "madness" and his self-identification with Renfield imply (p. 118), Seward himself is corrupted by wasteland duality. As we've heard, he has "sucked" Van Helsing's blood; his mansion embodies a split-personality, and he later betrays a vampirish "savage delight" (p. 232) in contemplating the behead-

[18] In *Backgrounds to Victorian Literature,* ed, by Richard Levine (San Francisco: Chandler Publishing Co., 1967), p. 126.

ing of his one-time beloved, Lucy. Significantly, his "branch of science" is "brain knowledge"—that "vital aspect—the knowledge of the brain" (p. 78); and very early he confesses that his own personality is guided both by "unconscious cerebration" and its "conscious brother." (p. 76). At its best, such Jekyll-Hydeism allows him to see that his homocidal, "unhallowed work" against Dracula ironically comes under the "perils of the law" (p. 219) of the parochial, Victorian penal code. On the other hand, at its most repressive, this dualism renders him a doubting Thomas, willing to convict the "abnormally clever" Van Helsing as the vampire (pp. 223-24). Moreover, his sexual repression is clearly evident when, as "sperm" drips from the candle onto Lucy's coffin, he considers the ghoulish business "as much an affront to the dead as it would have been to have stripped off her clothing in her sleep while living" (p. 217). However, when Seward finally accepts the "dual life" (p. 220) of Lucy, he symbolically (like, presumably, the Victorian reader) also accepts his own.

If Seward is alter-ego for the reader as detached spectator, Jonathan Harker, who begins the novel on an "unknown night-journey" (p. 12), is a "sufficient substitute" (p. 19) for the reader as actively questing knight-errant.[19] In this sense, his name *(Hark!)* flashes a danger-signal or caveat to the Victorian audience lest it too fall victim to the arid beliefs of the wasteland —especially close-minded legalisms since Harker, as London solicitor, allegorically represents the Law. Moreover, his development as scapegoat-quester places him within that favorite nineteenth-century genre, the *Bildungsroman.* He thus is also descendant of the prototypical British slayer of monsters as he arrives in Transylvania on "the eve of St. George's Day" (p. 5). His letter of reference from Mr. Hawkins to the Count provides a fitting prologue to his development since it praises his life-saving faith but also implies his vulnerable innocence and renders suspect the Victorian definition of "manhood": "He is a young man, full of energy and talent in his own way, and of a very faithful disposition. He is discreet and silent and has grown into manhood in my service" (p. 19).

[19]For the relevance of the questing-knight of Romance theme to "Romantic" literature, see...Harold Bloom, "The Internalization of Quest-Romance," *Yale Review,* LVIII (Summer 1969), 526-36.

Thus he becomes Dracula's prisoner in the Perilous Castle "without that protection of the law" (p. 49) which had been his insulation against the realities of natural life. Here Harker's repression, "an agony of delightful anticipation" (p. 42), is most evident when he is nearly seduced by the three succubi in the awful daring of a moment's surrender. In this oneiro-vision, the sexual frustrations of the Victorian groom-to-be serve to prophetically link the blond succubus with his own intended, Mina: "I seemed to know her face, and to know it in connection with some dreamy fear, but I could not recollect at the moment how or where. ...I felt in my heart a wicked, burning desire that they would kiss me with those red lips. It is not good to note this down; lest some day it should meet Mina's eyes and cause her pain; but it is the truth" (p. 41). Such honesty ultimately saves Harker; and even after he suppresses that Transylvanian experience, he still believes his earlier conviction: "I *must* know the truth" (p. 44, italics Stoker's). Throughout the novel, this Galahad-figure's fate tacitly hinges upon Dracula's, the Fisher King. When he finally returns to the Perilous Castle and with the phallic Kukri knife helps to slay Dracula (p. 416), Harker no longer "felt impotent" (p. 206) but reclaims the sexual prerogatives which Dracula had usurped and produces a new male heir on the very anniversary of the Count's ritualistic beheading and symbolic castration, or "sterilization." Stoker's own honesty here about Victorian sexual repression is reminiscent of Dickens' more fanciful version in *David Copperfield,* for when Uriah Heep (who David says "knew me better than I knew myself") gloats to David: "I love the ground my Agnes walks on," the young hero dreams that he snatches "a red hot...poker" from the fire and pierces "him through the body" and is repeatedly "haunted" by this fantasy (Chapt. 25). But Harker is more realistic (in both senses) than David; and as quester only he thematically unites cup and lance, or tomb and knife, renews the wasteland, and personally "wake[s] again to the realities of life" (p. 333).

As students are quick to point out, the early correspondence between Lucy and Mina seems to be the only "boring" section of the novel (though the overdrawn and somewhat anti-climactic conclusion is an actual flaw). However, the saccharine melodrama of this brief section creates an appropriate and ironic backdrop for the real horrors about to be visited upon the two girls and hence also serves to explode the life-denying conventions of Victorian sentimentality in whose wasteland, as Eliot implies, symbolic "death had undone so many." The repercussions of this shock further agitate the Victorian reader who has been conditioned to expect no danger for, or ambivalence from, a heroine named *Lucy,* the principle of right light. However, most simply the novel teaches that "There are darknesses in life, and there are lights" (p. 201). When this fiancée of Arthur betrays her "dual life" (p. 220), when "false Lucy" and "true Lucy" (p. 341) begin to merge, and when she becomes through the lifeblood of all her various donors a symbolic "polyandrist" and literal "Medusa" (p. 232), her role as Guinevere (etymologically "white" or "fair" lady), scapegoat of an unnatural and wasted courtly-love code, is clear. As Lucy's transformation indicates, the stereotyped Victorian woman, elevated on a pedestal or embowered in an ivory tower like the Lady of Shalott, denies belief in the life-giving forces of carnal nature and produces the wasteland nightmare: "She seemed like a nightmare of Lucy as she lay there; the pointed teeth, the bloodstained, voluptuous mouth—which it made one shudder to see—the whole carnal and unspiritual appearance, seeming like a devilish mockery of Lucy's sweet purity" (pp. 234-35).

However, if the blood of Dracula lethally drowns hitherto one-sided Lucy, it therapeutically baptizes, and provides rebirth for, diminutive *Mina*—Wilhelmina, the "resolute protectoress." In this sense, there are also two Minas in the novel. The early Mina, teacher of Victorian "etiquette and decorum" (p. 188), scoffs at the idea of the "New Woman" (p. 98), wishes to "build...castles in the air" (p. 59), and feels that her husband holding her arm in public is "improper" (p. 188). However, she grows from this emblem of angelic Victorian morality to the stature of the later Mina who possesses a "man's brain...and a woman's heart" (p. 258). Thus as androgynous Tiresias in the wasteland, her open-minded epistemology balances the close-minded gnoses of the vampire hunters: "her tender faith against all our fears and doubting" (p. 340). And of course it is when Mina embraces Dracula in what Seward terms "that terrible and horrid position" (p. 313), that she drinks his baptismal blood and restorative beliefs. This ichor, the "poison that distils itself out of good things" (p. 356), provides an antidote by a kind of homeopathic magic to wasteland sterility. And Mina is able to pass on this old new-life through the veins of her son. As psychopomp, her repeated slogan becomes a liberating epigraph for the theme of the entire novel: "There must be no concealment...Alas! we have had too much already" (p. 320).

Finally, Van Helsing and Dracula himself are both quite similar and represent vital, foreign imports which the insular Victorian creed must smuggle in for restoration of domestic tranquility. Like the Count, Van Helsing transfuses blood, has had his blood "sucked" by Seward, is an isolated, enigmatic personality, and is also the same kind of "master amongst men" (p. 353) that Dracula is. Indeed both vie in a psychomachia over Mina's soul; and Van Helsing even boasts of telepathic powers over the Count: "I, too, am wily; and I think his mind in a little while" (p. 340). Furthermore, as the Professor peripatetically instructs the others in the ways of vampirism (Hell-Singer?), his constant, thematic imperatives are "trust" and "believe." As Seward suggests:

> He is a seemingly arbitrary man, but this is because he knows what he is talking about better than anyone else. He is a philosopher and metaphysician, and one of the most advanced scientists of his day; and he has, I believe, an absolutely open mind. This, with an iron nerve, a temper of ice-brook, an indomitable resolution, self-command, and toleration exalted from virtues to blessings, and the kindliest and truest heart that beats—these form his equipment for the noble work that he is doing for mankind—work both in theory and practice, for his views are as wide as his all embracing sympathy (p. 123).

However, for all this learning and blessed virtue, Van Helsing, unlike the somewhat similar Mordecai in *Daniel Deronda,* is not an inhuman oracle; rather, as Seward fails to perceive, his personal life too has become a wasteland: "My life is a barren and lonely one, and so full of work that I have not had much time for friendships" (p. 203). Thus, Van Helsing's feet of human clay save him from becoming the type of foreign mentor, like Will Ladislaw in *Middlemarch,* so stereotypically common in Victorian fiction; and he is more like the sympathetic Herr Klesmer in *Daniel Deronda,* though much grander in scale than that music teacher.

In fact, he periodically breaks down under the strain of the psychomachia; "the very instinct of man" in him is sorely tempted by the "new emotion" of sex before the "voluptuous" succubi (p. 409); and he "tremble[s]" during his "butchery" (p. 410) of these vampiresses. And even this Merlin-figure was once a non-believer: "I admit that at first I was sceptic. Were it not that through long years I have train myself to keep an open mind, I could not have believe until such time as that fact thunder on my ear" (p. 260). Still armed with his Catholic faith, so foreign to low-church Protestantism, and his "open mind," he is the primary savior of the wasteland. His gospel finally becomes the redeeming deed of the novel: "I may err—I am but man; but I believe in all I do" (p. 181).

And lastly, Dracula. As villain, he transcends the run of the mill malice of such incarnation of Victorian vice as Alex D'Urbeville, Fagin, or George Eliot's Grandcourt although his sometime sneering humor often does echo them. As he taunts his anemic pursuers: "You think to baffle me, you—with your pale faces all in a row, like sheep in a butcher's. You shall be sorry yet, each of you! You think you have left me without a place to rest; but I have more. My revenge is just begun" (pp. 338-39). Still, Dracula's "revenge" brands him as Archetypal Rebel; and his role is much closer to Milton's Satan and his descendants, the nineteenth-century Prometheans—Manfred, Cain, Ahab, Frankenstein's Monster, and Heathcliff. As a matter of fact, as Demiurge or Rival of God, "this terrible and mysterious enemy" (p. 259) is compared to "Judas" (p. 55), but most often to "the Evil one" himself (p. 265); while Renfield's madness is illuminating enough to even call Dracula "God" (p. 296). However, as indicated throughout this essay, the Count is also an anachronistic Fisher King on his own black "quest" (p. 48) of "creeping into knowledge" (p. 334). His "child-brain," the primitive personality or Id, must be re-absorbed by the Victorian "man-brain"; and the Count himself must be "sterilis[ed]" (p. 328) and his literal *sang-froid* replaced with a new warm-blooded King for restoration of the wasteland. His crossing to London on the ship *Demeter* symbolically underscores this need for cyclic rebirth. Moreover, one of Dracula's opening speeches to Victorian Harker heralds his role as redeeming gnostic: "There is reason in all things as they are, and did you see with my eyes and know with my knowledge, you would perhaps better understand" (p. 23).

Finally, we hear that "There have been from the loins of this very one great men and good women" (p. 265); and this anticipates the sanguine birth of the Harker child through whose veins run not only the Victorian blood of his parents but also the vitality of the Count whose blood Mina has drunk. And this new, twentieth-century Fisher King, appropriately born on the anniversary of Dracula's death, not only represents the ancient blood-knowledge of his second father; but shoring these fragments against England's ruin, "his bundle of names links all" the allegorical epistemologies of the "little band of men together" (p. 218). The emphasis of the last sentences of the novel on acquired beliefs reveals the polynomial child's inherited, new knowledge: "We want no proofs; we ask none to *believe* us! This boy will some day *know* her sweetness and loving care; later on he will *understand* how some men so loved her that they did dare much for her sake" (p. 418, italics mine). And, we might add, he will *know* how much these Victorian "old knights of the Cross" dared "to redeem" the wasteland and "to set the world free" (pp. 354-55).

H. P. Lovecraft and an
American Literary Tradition

by Philip A. Shreffler

Much of the vitality of the literary tradition in America is derived from its being so intimately bound up in the horrific, the speculative, and the fantastic. It seems that a long, dark shadow of fantasy has always lain across our national literature — from the devil- and witch-ridden forests of the New England Puritans right up to the most contemporary American fabulists such as Kurt Vonnegut, Jr., Robert Coover, and Donald Barthelme. Along the way we have had the gothic tales of Charles Brockden Brown, the New York Dutch fantasies of Irving, the dark allegories of Hawthorne, and the more philosophical terror of Melville. Poe acquainted American literature with "the grim phantasm FEAR," and Oliver Wendell Holmes worked out his serpentine imagery in *Elsie Venner.* The nihilistic Ambrose Bierce, "Bitter Bierce" as he was sometimes called, produced what were perhaps the most caustic and cynical horror stories of the post-Civil War period.

Even when T. S. Eliot admitted us to the wasteland of the twentieth century, we found ourselves moving through a bizarre landscape that was at once strange and familiar. And it is certainly significant that one of the greatest American novels about the tragic defect in our national character, which we have come to call "the American Dream," was Fitzgerald's *The Great Gatsby,* the story of a man who inhabits a dream world almost exclusively, a dream world that is his undoing.

"H. P. Lovecraft and an American Literary Tradition" (editor's title). From *The H. P. Lovecraft Companion* by Philip A. Shreffler (Westport, Conn.: Greenwood Press, 1977), pp. 19-32. Used by permission of Greenwood Press.

To say that H. P. Lovecraft was a part of this literary and intellectual mainstream would be in error; his literary intent was essentially only to write tales of terror. But it would be equally erroneous to suggest that Lovecraft was not affected by the mainstream's currents or to say that there is nothing American about his work. In fact, Lovecraft's fiction, and particularly his late or mature fiction, is very American in character.

Lovecraft was raised by his mother and then his two aunts in the essential belief that he was a kind of aristocrat, that is, a gentleman of an old New England family who did not associate with the rabble. It is reasonable to assume, therefore, that he was to some degree divorced from the mainstream of American life. It would not, however, be reasonable to say that the Puritan morality that still influences most Americans did not influence Lovecraft as well. It is just that in Lovecraft's life and fiction that influence manifested itself in a way different from those of other major American writers.

Throughout American history, the simplistic Puritan dichotomy of good against evil, black versus white, as it was often symbolized, caused a kind of national neurosis. The tension created by this Manichean division has shown itself from Puritan times to the present in the notion that what is not godly, or good at least, is automatically shameful or wicked. While Lovecraft subscribed for much of his life to the idea that blacks were an inferior race and that the luridness of sex had no place in the minds of genteel people, the dark-versus-light dichotomy is not used in a Puritan manner in his fiction.

Although the dark-light metaphor appears regularly throughout American literature, the two greatest writers to make use of it were Hawthorne and Melville. Hawthorne's bleak tales employed this Puritan notion to deepen our understanding of the principles of dark and light that exist in every human heart quite independent of any external God or devil. The God or devil of men is of their own creation and depends upon what choices a man makes within his own sphere of experience. Hawthorne felt that human beings usually opt for wicked choices, those that are ruinous of love and destructive to any warmth that humans might share in an impossibly difficult world.

For Melville the dark-light imagery took on universal proportions and finally became contradictory and ambiguous. It is the dark Captain Ahab who hunts the White Whale, but Ahab sees Moby Dick as inscrutably malevolent and wishes to destroy him. Through it all the whale, whom Ishmael has described as ghastly in its whiteness for a variety of philosophical reasons, seems to remain benign, or at least resists the reader's attempts to understand it as good or evil.

But the point is that for both of these writers, the dark-light conflict exists within the personalities or the souls of the major characters. In Lovecraft it is different. Here the theme of good versus evil within the hero usually does not surface—and when it does, it is in the form of a shocking recognition of the existence of evil alone (as in Charles Dexter Ward's being obsessed by the spirit of his ancestor Joseph Curwin), a condition that often drives the main character to suicide, as with Arthur Jermyn. Normally, however, the evil experienced by Lovecraft's main characters is external to them and is pervasive in the world. This causes a terrible understanding of the nature of things, which, once again, may lead to suicide.

In this respect, Lovecraft is strikingly modern. The sense of being alone and afraid in a world one never made is common among many writers of the twentieth century. We shall probably never know whether or not Lovecraft was making an apt pun in the title of "Arthur Jermyn"—whether or not he was trying to tell his readers just how germane this tale is to his thinking. But it surely is.

In the first paragraph of the story, Lovecraft writes that:

> Science, already oppressive with its shocking revelations, will perhaps be the ultimate exterminator of our human species—if separate species we be—for its reserve of unguessed horrors could never be borne by mortal brains if loosed upon the world. If we knew what we are, we should do as Arthur Jermyn did; and Arthur Jermyn soaked himself in oil and set fire to his clothing one night.

This is a singularly powerful and affecting passage. It has all of the brutal and forceful frontal-attack qualities that one might associate with a photograph of an assassination, as well as the lean, spare, tough literary technique found in the best twentieth-century writers.

If all this sounds prophetic of our own times on Lovecraft's part, we should keep in mind that it is not. Between the years 1900 and 1905, the world, as it had been known up to that time, simply ceased to exist. During this period, the Wright Brothers flew their gasoline-powered aeroplane at Kitty Hawk, Sigmund Freud published *On the Interpretations of Dreams,* a book that shattered man's image of himself, and Albert Einstein brought the great age of Newtonian physics to an end with the publication of his *Special Theory of Relativity.*

Lovecraft, of course, was keenly interested in science, and by the time he came to write those lines in "Authur Jermyn," he had already witnessed, as had so many others, the horrors of the Great War—a war so terrible that it was thought by some to be man's final war. The world of 1900 through 1920 was a world that seemed to be falling apart, a chaos that pointed the way toward Armageddon. In "Arthur Jermyn," a story of a human being who had not quite "let go the hot gorilla's paw" (as Ray Bradbury put it in *Something Wicked This Way Comes*), Lovecraft was simply responding sensitively and cynically to the world that he saw.

There are two biographical factors here that are important. First, there was Lovecraft's physical isolation from the outside world, a situation that must have profoundly deepened his acid scorn for the human race and the doomed world it inhabits. And second, although raised in a Puritanical home and influenced psychologically by it to his very roots, Lovecraft was affected enough by modern science to have become an agnostic. With the removal of a religious framework in terms of which to see a redemptive moral salvation for man, things must have seemed pointless and bleak indeed.

The question may arise to whether or not Lovecraft's strange half-breeds, the offspring of horrible liaisons between men and monsters, can be seen as a return to the nineteenth-century tension between dark and light principles existing simultaneously in a human being. Here we may think of the people of Innsmouth, of Dunwich's Wilbur Whately, of Arthur Jermyn himself. But we seem to arrive once again at the pessimistic conclusion. In these characters, though mixtures of men and monsters, it is the evil of the monster and the evil of the human parent that survive. In those cases in which Lovecraft surrounds a decent and pure main character (many of his first-person narrators are modeled upon himself) with wicked ones, it is the sheer enormity of the world's evil pitted against the pitiful insignificance of the hero's good that drives the hero into madness or actually into removing himself from the world by violence. There is a clearly perceivable paranoia in this version of reality.

Finally, and this is perhaps the most insidious dimension of Lovecraft's work, we come to understand that if we are looking for a moral, we might just as well forget it. There is none. This was a view taken by the post-Civil War naturalists who wrote in the generation preceding Lovecraft's. Represented by literary artists such as Stephen Crane, Jack London, Frank Norris, and Ambrose Bierce, the naturalists saw the universe as a blind, dead, uncaring beast that occasionally blundered against men and, without any particular malice, exterminated them. This kind of thing happens often in Lovecraft, particularly in the earlier stories like "The Other Gods," in which it is the encounter with monsters, which are only innocently going about their business of being monsters, that destroys men.

In the later stories, however, the monsters do take on malevolent characteristics and become creatures whose design it is to wipe out mankind and inherit the earth. This notion is pure survival-of-the-fittest philosophy (which is to say in this case survival of the most powerful), another scientific idea that rocked the world and has been around in one form or another ever since.

One way, therefore, that Lovecraft's literary career might be categorized is by dividing it according to whether or not the forces of nature and supernature that appear in the stories operate through naturalistic impersonality or through conscious evil intent. It is generally in the early stories that we find the former and in the later Mythos pantheon stories that we find the latter. This method of division, of course, does not account for many of the pure fantasy-land or dream stories, such as "The Doom That

Came to Sarnath," which...conform to the Dunsanian poetic principle.

Of the prodigious amount of writing that Lovecraft did, it was surely his so-called Cthulhu Mythos for which he became most famous. Briefly, the Mythos consists of a series of a dozen or so stories, interrelated but not interdependent, that are based upon a common, central theme. The idea is that before man ever evolved upon the earth, a race of creatures that Lovecraft called the Great Old Ones came here from deep space to rule. But they were essentially demonic in nature, and when man came upon the earth, they subjugated him. Some men in turn fell to worshiping these creatures. Subsequently, the Old Ones lapsed in their rule and either fell into a dreamless slumber in the earth's remote places or vanished into other dimensions of space and time.

But the seed of evil had either been planted in man by the Old Ones, or it had existed already. In any case, by using certain horrible rituals that survived from the Old Ones' reign on earth, small enclaves of human beings remained dedicated to the Old Ones, virtually forming a religion of the basis of their return. And it was through those surviving rituals found in books like the *Necronomicon* that the Old Ones' reinheritance of the earth could be effected.

This theory is particularly well developed in "The Case of Charles Dexter Ward," in which Lovecraft suggests that every element of what we have come to call the black arts has its roots in the ritual veneration of these monsters from space. And the theory is especially provocative and intriguing in that it attempts to unify and attribute a common cause to human superstition and occultism—something that certain psychologists and anthropologists have been trying to do for years anyway.

A point to take into consideration here is the naming of the Cthulhu Mythos. Actually, Lovecraft himself never used this term, referring instead only to his "Cthulhuism" or "Yog-Sothothery." The term "Cthulhu Mythos" was only invented, or at least came into popular use, after his death. This was largely the doing of his literary friends and disciples. We ought to remember, however, that in the pantheon of gods that Lovecraft incorporated into his Mythos, Cthulhu was only the sea god who dwelt in the submarine depths of R'lyeh, an Atlantis-like setting. Other gods include Yog-Sothoth (hence, "Yog-Sotho-thery"), Shub-Niggurath, Azathoth, and Nyarlathotep.

All of these creatures are mentioned in one or more stories, but it is only in "The Call of Cthulhu' that Cthulhu actually appears. The reason, then, for naming the myth cycle after Cthulhu is a bit of a mystery. And it is really a trifle unfortunate, since it not only underplays the importance of the others (like Yog-Sothoth, whose offspring rips up the countryside in "The Dunwich Horror") but also tends to distract us from one truly significant element that most of the stories have in common—the New England setting.

Although the list of stories that can be considered Mythos tales varies from critic to critic, it can hardly be disallowed that the majority of them take place against the Puritan setting of Lovecraft's beloved New England. The use of the term "Cthulhu Mythos" draws our attention away from this fact (in "The Call of Cthulhu" the monster appears in the South Seas) and directs us either to Cthulhu's watery domain or to the god himself.

But...Lovecraft's use of the New England setting is of paramount importance to his literary theory, and it is for this reason that we probably ought to use the term "New England Mythos" to refer to that particular series of stories. However, to avoid needless confusion this series will be referred to here simply as the Mythos stories. And whether New England or Cthulhu, the Mythos stories surely stand independent of generic controversy.

One of the traditional criteria that scholars and critics of literature (and particularly of American literature) have applied to determine the merit of a serious writer's work is to consider to what extent that writer understood the literary history of which he was a part. Here, specifically, we are dealing with Lovecraft not only as a writer of fantastic fiction but of American fantastic fiction.

Of remarkable significance to this study of Lovecraft's literary theory is his observation that "Quite alone as both a novel and a piece of terror-literature stands the famous *Wuthering Heights* (1847) by Emily Brontë, with its mad vistas of bleak, wind-swept

Yorkshire moors and the violent, distorted lives they foster." From this it is obvious that setting is highly integral to plot in Lovecraft's estimation. Furthermore, holding *Wuthering Heights* in such high esteem, singling it out from other British Romantic literature, has been a kind of preoccupation with American writers and critics, for the elements of American romance are nowhere more evident in a British novel than in Brontë's book. These elements would include the large-scale setting of the open moor country and the skillful commingling of the actual and the imaginary to a point where it is difficult for the reader to discern the difference.

In grappling with the problem of American horror fiction, Lovecraft includes a lengthy section in *Supernatural Horror in Literature* entitled "The Weird Tradition in America," which contains full and detailed discussions of Nathaniel Hawthorne and Ambrose Bierce, whom Lovecraft considered of particular importance to the genre. The one notable figure missing in this discussion is Herman Melville, author of *Moby-Dick,* with its diabolism and satanic implications, as well as of a number of short stories that qualify as weird fiction. But this may be accounted for when we remember that *Moby-Dick,* one of the greatest and most profound American novels, was not recognized as anything but a sea story until the early twentieth century, and at the time Lovecraft wrote his essay, little critical work had been done on the book.

Lovecraft does indicate his familiarity with some American literary criticism, however, since he cites the scholar Paul Elmer More in the essay's examination of Hawthorne. Lovecraft had probably read the two excellent essays on Hawthorne in More's famous *Shelburne Essays in American Literature,* and later Lovecraft was able to mobilize D. H. Lawrence's observations about Hawthorne from his *Studies in Classic American Literature.* What this shows is that Lovecraft was not simply making idle, armchair, belletristic observations about American literature but had engaged in its serious study.

Paraphrasing More's work, Lovecraft perceptively points to the all-important cultural context into which American literature was born. America was, he says, deeply marked by "keen spiritual and theological interests" from the time of the first Separatist landing at Plymouth Rock. This, coupled with the desolate scene of virgin wilderness into which the Separatists had been carried by the *Mayflower,* caused the Puritan leader William Bradford to write that his people felt cut off—three thousand miles of ocean behind them and in front of them "a hideous and desolate wilderness, full of wild beasts and wild men. ... For summer being done, all things stand upon them with a weather-beaten face, and the whole country, full of woods and thickets, represented a wild and savage hue." Bradford noted that under such circumstances the Puritans could turn their eyes only upward toward heaven, and this represents the first American impulse to escape physical reality for a spiritual reality, and established the propensity to transcend to finer, more shining worlds.

The Puritans considered that much of what was earthly was satanic. In this way the Indians were associated with the devil, and the conditions were set up under which operated the celebrated Salem witchcraft trials and executions that weighed so heavily on Hawthorne, whose own ancestor had been one of the prosecutors. Hawthorne himself did not believe in these Puritan interpretations of nature, but he did use them symbolically in his investigation of man's moral constitution. Lovecraft's judgment is wholly correct that Hawthorne

> grieved at an unmoral universe which everywhere transcends the conventional patterns thought by our forefathers to represent divine and immutable law. Evil, a very real force to Hawthorne, appears on every hand as a lurking, conquering adversary; and the visible world becomes in his fancy a theatre of infinite tragedy and woe, with unseen half-existent influences hovering over and through it, battling for supremacy and moulding the destinies of the hapless mortals who form its vain and self-deluded population. *The heritage of American weirdness was his to a most intense degree, and he saw a dismal throng of vague spectres behind the common phenomona of life. ...* [My italics.]

This Platonic notion of a shadowy world beyond or behind common day-to-day occurrences runs as a strong current throughout American literature. Lovecraft was not only wise to observe it but knew enough about is literary validity to use it in his own fiction. The demonic cults and hidden evils that fester behind the facade of those New England villages in his stories are a clear manifestation of his use of this philosophical concept.

For Lovecraft, "foremost as a finished, artistic unit among all our author's weird material is the famous and exquisitely wrought novel, *The House of Seven Gables. ...*" Actually, this, like Hawthorne's other three long fiction works, is by definition not a novel, but a Romance. In defining the Romance genre, Hawthorne wrote in "The Custom-House" that the Romance establishes "a neutral territory, somewhere between the real world and fairy-land, where the Actual and the Imaginary may meet and each imbue itself with the nature of the other." In the preface to *The House of Seven Gables* Hawthorne adds that a writer of Romance "wishes to claim a certain latitude, both as to its fashion and material, which he would not have felt himself entitled to assume had he professed to be writing a Novel." The Romance writer may "so manage his atmospherical medium as to bring out or mellow the lights and deepen and enrich the shadows of the picture." In Lovecraft, too, it is the skillful management of "his atmospherical medium" that makes the stories so successful as vehicles for drawing out hidden and uncertain sensations of fear.

In the twilight world of the Romance it is precisely what one does not see, or rather what one is uncertain about seeing, that lends to it an atmosphere of terror. In Hawthorne's "Young Goodman Brown," for example, Brown never actually sees a witch flying on a broomstick as he travels through the forest on his way to a witch's sabbath. The old man who is his guide carries a walking stick that *seems* to turn into a serpent, but in the half-light Brown cannot be certain. Similarly, in Lovecraft it is often what he does not tell us that creates the uncanny atmosphere. Lovecraft's weakest moments tend to be those in which he describes a monster visually; and his strongest ones, those in which he only hints dimly at what may be lurking nearby. Like the rampant imaginations of Hawthorne's guilt-ridden characters, the imaginations of Lovecraft's readers fill in what Lovecraft has deliberately left out, but they fill it in vaguely, so that they themselves may not be quite aware of what is causing their uneasiness.

Unlike Hawthorne, however, Lovecraft was little interested in dealing with life on a moral level, except in isolated instances such as in "The White Ship," which is a moral allegory, pure and simple, based on *Pilgrim's Progress* and possibly on Hawthorne's "The Celestial Railroad." Hawthorne's theme of ancestral evil descending upon an unfortunate victim who must then wrestle with the moral issue becomes transmuted in Lovecraft. Although he uses this idea in many of his stories, he uses it as the stimulus that evokes only terror in his main characters. Usually, in Lovecraft's mature work, the main characters find themselves caught in a universe of cosmic conspiracy, in a world that is impossibly evil and bent only on the destruction of men. In this way Lovecraft's fiction becomes strangely nihilistic, akin to that of Bierce.

Bierce,who wandered into Mexico in 1913 and was never seen again, is best remembered for his tales of horror and his bitter Civil War stories. In the latter category the best known are "An Occurrence at Owl Creek Bridge," "Chickamauga," and "One of the Missing," social and psychological antiwar statements both grim and upsetting. Of his horror stories "The Damned Thing" is perhaps most often read, and it is in this tale that Lovecraft sees Bierce's sense of "inhumanity" finding "vent in a rare strain of sardonic comedy and graveyard humour." An example, says Lovecraft, is illustrated in the subtitles, "such as 'One does not always eat what is on the table,' describing a body laid out for a coroner's inquest, and 'A man though naked may be in rags,' referring to a frightfully mangled corpse."

These philosophical questions aside, however, it was to Poe that Lovecraft owed the most as a prose stylist and Poe whom he revered more than any other American writer. In *Supernatural Horror in Literature* Lovecraft devotes an entire section to Poe, which occurs between "Special Literature on the Continent" and "The Weird Tradition in America," suggesting not only the importance of Poe, but also that he was Lovecraft's link between Europe (where Poe was appreciated and read during his lifetime) and America.

Lovecraft saw Poe as rising to heights of "cosmic terror" far above that which was achieved by any other author of weird fiction, adding that it was "to our good fortune as Americans" to be able to claim Poe as our own. The great similarities between Poe and Lovecraft form the kelson of Lovecraft's literary theory and thus demand scrutiny here.

Fortunately, in addition to his fiction and poetry Poe also wrote "The Philosophy of Composition," an excellent essay on his own literary theory. In that essay Poe notes that fiction writing usually begins with a thesis or a basic idea for a plot, and this, in turn, is filled in "with description, dialogue, or authorial comment. ..." Poe, however, prefers "commencing with the consideration of an *effect.*" Poe says to himself. "Of the innumerable effects, or impressions, of which the heart, the intellect, or (more generally) the soul is susceptible, what one on the present occasion shall I select?'" The effect on his readers of a story or poem, he decides, must be *"universally* appreciable."

In an all-important definitive passage, Poe observes:

> That pleasure which is at once the most intense, the most elevating, and the most pure, is, I believe, found in the contemplation of the Beautiful. When, indeed, men speak of beauty, they mean, precisely, not a quality, as is supposed, but an effect—they refer, in short, just to that intense and pure elevation of *soul, not* of intellect, or of heart. ... which is experienced in consequence of contemplating "the beautiful."

"Beauty," Poe maintains, "is the excitement, or pleasurable elevation, of the soul."

But for Poe the soul's elevation being pleasurable did not preclude the aesthetic experience of fear or unhappiness, since even these excite and elevate the soul to new levels of sensation. Therefore, Poe concludes that if this elevation of the soul must be universally appreciated, he should employ a tone in his work that is the summit of spiritual excitation. This, he believes, is sadness. The next question is: Of all melancholy topics which is the most melancholy? His answer is "the death of a beautiful woman," since death and sexual beauty are likely to provoke the greatest sympathetic reaction in the reader. Hence we have "The Raven," "Ligeia," and "The Fall of the House of Usher," all of which reflect this concept.

Poe then builds upon the concept by choosing just the imagery and the heavy, Latinate phrasing framed by the proper plot structure to convey the effect he has chosen. Like the artistic Prince Prospero in "The Masque of the Red Death," Poe himself has that "wonderful eye for colors and effects" that combine subtly to affect the reader. In "The Fall of the House of Usher," for example, it is Roderick Usher's obsession with fear ("the grim phantasm FEAR," he calls it) that culminates in the reader's own experience of fear.

Lovecraft has been much criticized for his apparent disinterest in strong, flashy elements of plot. Indeed, plot is sometimes so de-emphasized that one may read forty pages or so of one of the longer stories in the course of which nothing much happens. But Lovecraft well understood what he was about. These long passages often amount to virtually Henry James-like descriptions of the main character's psychological state or are given to physical depictions of setting. And it is this, rather than plot, that contributes to the total effect in Lovecraft's fiction. By focusing analytically on a man whose psychological state is deteriorating, Lovecraft is echoing Poe's treatment of the mind of Roderick Usher, and this technique casts an eerie and ghastly shadow over the entire work.

As an aside here, a basic difference between Poe and Lovecraft should be noted. While for Poe the most effective emotional theme was the death of a beautiful woman, Lovecraft almost completely eschewed the introduction of women into his fiction. The only story wherein a woman figures prominently is "The Thing on the Doorstep," and actually it is only Asenath Waite's physical presence that is the vehicle for horror, not any malevolence of the feminine mind. There has been a great deal of speculation about latent homosexuality on Lovecraft's part because of his disinclination to write about women. But this theory is better left in the hands of armchair psychologists and Freudian critics. A far more plausible reason for Lovecraft's aversion may be found in his Puritan upbringing and his lack of experience with women. After all, it is fairly difficult to write about something to which one has had little exposure and that one simply does not understand.

Following the lead of both Poe and Hawthorne, Lovecraft also came to understand the absolute importance of setting in achieving an overall effect. Hawthorne had struggled with the problem of a usable American setting in which the romance landscape could be constructed. He firmly believed that settings had to be in concert with the weird psychophysical action of a story or long fiction work. But America, he lamented, was simply too young a nation to have the appropriate gothic appurtenances necessary for the Romance. Nevertheless, Hawthorne reached for as dark and ancient a past as he could find. It was natural for him to use the haunted, half-lit world of the New England Puritans as setting. Poe, rather than resorting to New England, preferred to dislocate his setting in space and time, remaining unclear about just where the action was taking place.

Lovecraft borrowed from both authors, sometimes, like Poe, employing a setting "out of Space and out of Time," or, like Hawthorne, using colonial New England as his fantastic frame of reference. This latter impulse is what gave rise to Lovecraft's inventing the wild, desolate villages of Arkham, Kingsport, Dunwich, and Innsmouth as fictive locales. And it is these settings, as much as any monster-god he created, that have captured the imagination of his followers. Lovecraft's repetitive use of these settings has indeed had such an effect as to convince many readers that they are real places. That Arkham or Dunwich cannot be found on a roadmap of Massachusetts is a common, confused observation of the neophyte reader of Lovecraft.

Finally, every bit as important as setting and the psychological examination of characters is Lovecraft's rhetorical style. It was, perhaps, through his attempts to imitate the heavily ornate style of Poe, as well as his exposure to British literature, that Lovecraft found himself given to immensely complex sentence structure and an archaic vocabulary. It has been said that readers are simply unable to deal with this, a charge also leveled at Henry James. Actually, Lovecraft almost certainly had less control over his diction than either Poe or James did, and his adjectival explosions and archaicisms often make his fiction sound a bit silly by comparison. What must be kept in mind here is not the frequent awkwardness and heavy-handedness of a given passage or set of passages but, rather, the cumulative *effect* of Lovecraft's stories—their weirdness, which is precisely what he wanted them to be invested with.

Perhaps this quality simply defies analysis; perhaps we should not analyze it. It should, however, be sufficient to say that it is exactly Lovecraft's rhetorical excesses that make his style consistent with his characters who feel madness growing on them against the backdrop of macabre, otherworldly settings. And this is the reason that strangely, and often against our will, we begin to feel that Lovecraft is not writing fiction, but a hideous version of truth.

In terms of Lovecraft's philosophical conception of his own work, then, we may see that he derived his understanding of what weird fiction must do primarily from Poe, and his sense of a usable American past and of a workable psychophysical landscape from Hawthorne's theory of the Romance. But in a larger way Lovecraft's most important contribution to the overall framework of American literature was not altogether derivative. In the early twentieth century, a time when the older modes of literary thought were crumbling and when a writer like Hemingway could successfully machine-gun his readers with staccato diction and syntax, Lovecraft stood firmly in the midst of a syntax that was meant to be woven magically around the reader. And although the fantastic strain in American literature will probably always exist in one form or another, the Romance form in America as it was understood and practiced by both Hawthorne and Poe all but vanished with Lovecraft's death. Lovecraft was the last American writer to guide us, in the nineteenth-century tradition, on a fearful torchlight tour of witch-haunted New England.

Anthropology, Fiction, and the Occult:
The Case of Carlos Castaneda

by David Murray

Carlos Castaneda's work has already gained attention from many different quarters as a form of anthropology, but I want here, by looking at some of Castaneda's stylistic devices, and by relating his books to some other best-sellers of the same period, to suggest another way of approaching his work—namely, as a slowly unfolding occult fiction.

Castaneda's books were first treated—and often still are—as a contribution to the growing anthropological literature on the use of hallucinogens. His approach was seen as innovatory in its stress on the anthropologist's *participation* in the drug experiences, and, even more crucially, in the way that the books attempt, by throwing the anthropologist's own attitudes into question, to communicate to the reader the full force of Don Juan's belief in a "separate reality." Anthropologists have either liked it and praised it for these qualities, or suspected its authenticity and rejected it.[1] Edward Spicer, for instance, an authority on the Yacqui Indians, and Mary Douglas broadly approved of it, and found the approach one to be encouraged,

"Anthropology, Fiction, and the Occult: The Case of Carlos Castaneda" by David Murray. Written for this collection, and printed by permission of the author.

[1]Daniel C. Noel has collected most of the important initial reactions in *Seeing Castaneda* (New York: Putnam's, 1976). Robert de Mille's witty and highly critical assessment, *Castaneda's Journey* (Santa Barbara: Capra Press, 1976) assembles the substantial evidence for seeing the books as a hoax, though not therefore valueless. Specific aspects of Castaneda are taken up in Nevill Drury's *Don Juan, Mescalito, and Modern Magic: The Mythology of Inner Space* (London: Routledge & Kegan Paul, 1978) and David Silverman's *Reading Castaneda* (London: Routledge & Kegan Paul, 1975).

whereas Weston La Barre and Edmund Leach smelled a rat from
the beginning. What everyone was clear about, though, was that
it was not Yacqui ethnography. There is hardly any detail given
of Don Juan's background or culture, and in each successive book
the encounter between the acolyte and the master becomes increasingly isolated and archetypal. It was pointed out, for instance, that in spite of all Castaneda's apprenticeship, and the
time apparently spent collecting and identifying herbs and fungi,
only the three best-known psychotropic substances are ever
named. Because, too, of the special position of Castaneda as
sorcerer's apprentice, rather than detached observer, we do not
have any overall view, whether functional or structural, of the
role of the experience of a "separate reality" in a *community*.
Where, for instance, Evans-Pritchard treats magic as inseparable
from a set of practices and beliefs in a community, gaining its
validity from its relation to them, we are forced here into a subjective experience which is increasingly ambiguous. The isolated
and noncultural aspects are accentuated and the social function
and role of the shaman—Don Juan's curing role, for instance—
are mostly ignored. *Power,* then, of a kind which is both personal
and supernatural but without any social dimension, is the issue
here, and Edmund Leach accurately pinpoints the romantic connections and origins: "The general tone is Coleridge—de Quincy
by Rousseau out of eighteenth-century Gothik" (Noel, p. 33). It
is this aspect of the books which I would suggest accounts for their
vast popularity, and it is interesting to compare them with some
other campus best-sellers in order to explore the implications of
this power and the master-disciple relationship in which it
operates.

The supposed liberation from rationality and its imposed
categories took many forms in the 1960s, and the interest in the
fantastic and occult has continued to grow, but it is important to
distinguish between the real possibilities for creative and utopian
speculation which fantasy, in the form of the invention of imaginary worlds, can represent, and the instrumentalization of
fantasy—the use of the irrational only to confirm the categories
of society, thereby providing only the *illusion* of an alternative.[2]

[2]See Jack Zipes, *Breaking the Magic Spell* (London: Heinemann, 1979).

The distinction between the two uses of the fantastic may be difficult to define, but it is notable how many of the most popular cult books of the 1960s counterculture involve a very clear master-pupil relationship and how many are concerned with the acquisition of a significantly amorphous or undefined power. Clearly this relates closely to the increase in actual religious practices and cults embodying this power relationship, and Weston La Barre asks the relevant question: "Is not the endless quest for a *guru* in fact diagnostic of the authoritarian personality, a sign of eternal adolescence in the seeker? That is, such persons dependently seek in the mere authority of other persons what can only be found in fresh inquiries of That Which Is, reality" (Noel, p. 40). I am pointing not to the increase in concern for the spiritual teachings of individuals here, but the way the quest is centered around ideas of personal power. The phenomenal popularity of Herman Hesse[3] among American students and the success of Fowles's novel *The Magus,* for instance, are as relevant to Castaneda's reception as is the spate of interest in traditional American Indian religion—although note that even here it is often centered around individuals: *Black Elk Speaks, Rolling Thunder, Lame Deer, Seeker of Visions.*[4] The idea that power and enlightenment are achieved *outside* one's community, in an isolation broken only by a confrontation with a primitive or alien individual, has a long pedigree in classic American literature,[5] but it also relates closely to the fundamental situation of anthropology, which can also be seen to embody a quest structure, as Vincent Crapanzano has pointed out:

> Whether consciously or unconsciously, the ethnographic experience is necessarily structured as a quest, and is subject to the forms of the quest, including the possibility, the necessity even, of temptation and revelation. It is this quest structure which may help to

[3]According to Robert Galbreath, New Directions had sold 1½ million copies of *Siddhartha* by 1970. For useful bibliographical information see Galbreath's essay in *Journal of Popular Culture,* Vol. V, No. 3, 1971, pp. 727-28.

[4]Ronald Sukenick's novel *Out* (Chicago: Swallow Press, 1973), includes a typical encounter with a Sioux medicine man which I take to be a gentle parody of this countercultural concern.

[5]See Leslie Fiedler's *Love and Death in the American Novel* (New York: Stein and Day, 1966), among others.

explain the anthropologist's—and his reader's—fascination with such phenomena as initiation rites, shamanistic voyages, the secret vision quests, and ritual revelations. It is also this quest structure that inevitably distorts the reality which is that of everyday life and which is in fact the subject matter of anthropology. Life is not, except perhaps for the most romantic, a quest. Social and cultural life are not necessarily structured around the possibility of inner, deep, profound, "heavy" meaning. Such is the concern of the anthropologist and again his reader, who are the offspring of a deeply disillusioned society "in quest" of more meaningful experience (provided, of course, that it is of easy access).[6]

There are further connections to be made with the traditional concerns of American literature. As has often been pointed out, the basic confrontation and communication in that literature is between *men,* and women are negative forces. The power which can be gained is ruined by women, it seems. Like hunting magic (and so often in American literature it *is* hunting, whether whales, bears, or deer, around which the power centers), which traditionally excludes women, the power of the "warrior" as it is described in Castaneda must be protected from being dissipated in the social or commonplace: Personal power can be stored up and generated when one's mind ceases to revolve around the petty arguments and issues of one's life, and one can suspend this superficial dialogue with oneself. It is not only *internal* dialogue which must be suspended, though, but one's social being. What we have, then, is power entirely outside the concerns of the social world (and therefore *without* meaningful moral dimensions, in spite of the constant use of general but empty terms like *good* and *evil* in Castaneda and so much literature of the occult) which feeds the fantasy of power without sympathy or humanity. The greatest exploration of this theme is not to be found in Herman Hesse (though *Magister Ludi* could perhaps offer, if properly read, an antidote to some of the excesses of the cult of spiritual quest and power generated by his other work) but *Moby Dick,* where the claims of occult Faustian power are set against both the losses incurred — the personal becomes impersonal — and alternative forms of knowledge, like that gained from Queequeg rather than Fedallah. In fact, the idea of *occult* non social power

[6]"Popular Anthropology," *Partisan Review,* Vol. 40, 1973, pp. 472-73.

is an interesting dimension to a well-worn critical theme in American literature.

The countercultural concern for the supernatural, though, often takes a different direction. It is an attempt to encompass, *within* the natural, areas which have been prematurely excluded by science and labeled as superstition, and Doug Boyd's *Rolling Thunder* provides an interesting comparison with Castaneda in this respect. Boyd's factual account of his meetings with a celebrated medicine man is concerned to demonstrate the validity of his views, and shows a lamentably uncritical acceptance of claims made for Rolling Thunder's powers, but it acts as a good indicator of the way in which rationality was being rejected in the name of a greater whole in the counterculture at large. Boyd clumsily counterattacks the arguments against the supernatural, for instance, in these terms:

> I had come to consider such a skill as Semu's [predictions based on observing bird behavior] truly scientific, an interpretation of complete and accurate observations in the light of countless years of accumulated data. Establishment whites would call it super-natural. How ironic that we who in a few short years have caused imbalance and turmoil among nearly all natural things should have conjured up a word like "supernatural" to label so much of the basic phenomena that we have chosen to ignore. Indians were the most natural of people, and the most supernatural people in the world might well be found among white establishment technologists who, as far as nature is concerned, know so little and still have manipulated so much."[7]

"Natural" here is being used as an empty word of praise, and "supernatural" is equated with "unnatural." Clearly, in this view the shaman's powers, whether actual or illusory, form *part* of this world, just a part we have ignored. There is no other source of power, no occult science, only a larger conception of the natural. This approach accounts for a great deal of the modern concern for the paranormal, with its broad ecological and holistic assumptions about the natural world and its relation to a development of psychological insights from Jung rather than behaviorism, but it seems to me that all of this approach has the effect finally

[7]*Rolling Thunder* (New York: Dell, 1974), p. 233.

of denying the occult, in the sense of an intrusion of another and alien reality into our own. Boyd's book exists in a social world much more than Castaneda's, and when the two books are compared, the bareness of Castaneda's and also the much greater sophistication of his writing are clear. The quality of writing is crucial here, in that it leads one to a consideration of the work not as anthropology or social document but as occult fiction. This may seem cavalier, but from the first, many readers—Joyce Carol Oates, Robert Bly, and Ronald Sukenick, among others—have recognized either the incorporation of techniques of fiction or the marks of an entirely fictive enterprise.

Castaneda begins in *The Teachings of Don Juan* with the recounting of experience under hallucinogenic drugs administered and supervised by Don Juan. This supervision is important because, as Castaneda elaborates in his structural analysis in the appendix, Don Juan's rules and his belief that there is a general pattern and a meaning to these experiences validates (gives the basis of a consensus to) what is being experienced by Castaneda. It may be drug-induced hallucination, but it is not meaningless or solipsistic. It is a world with its own set of rules and categories—and *power,* which can carry over into the "normal" world. If Castaneda's work had remained like this, it would be psychological and/or spiritual exploration, rather than occult, but the distinctive feature that begins to emerge in Castaneda, and which separates him from anthropology, is his building up of a carefully constructed narrative which has within it gaps, as well as bits of information which do not fit (How did he get to a particular place? Did he *really* fly? etc.) so that the *texture* of the narrative is supple and evasive. As soon as we get a *construction* of narrative like this, with its combination of a claim for verisimilitude and a concern for *shaping* the materials, we are in an area congruent with if not identical to fiction, regardless how much of it Castaneda actually experienced (at any level of reality). We can see a development here, over the course of the books, as the reliance on drugs to create the separate reality is given up. As long as drugs are involved it is easier to categorize the experiences as induced and remaining at the level of the psychological, however important the spiritual insights which result may be, but by the time we reach *Tales of Power* we are not allowed by the narrative to categorize the experiences as entirely psychological—we have a move toward the occult, in fact.

The occult necessarily distinguishes itself from fantasy by its insistence on the *intrusion* of the "other" into this world on this world's terms. That is, it has to be phenomenon-based. It is a curious contradiction, therefore, that the spiritual *proves* itself by the physical, or at least it is the physical phenomenon which provides the point of intersecting planes, crucial in an occult novel rather than a fantasy. The shift in Castaneda's work from psychological accounts (i.e., description of states of mind) to occult novel is shown in the different status accorded to the incursions of the nonordinary or separate reality into the ordinary. The crucial issue is whether it is corroborated by other external evidence. In the earlier works it is not, though it is understood and validated as a special and valuable sort of experience by Don Juan, but no claims beyond that are made, whereas in *Tales of Power* we have external corroboration to exclude the possibility of hallucination. An example will clarify this. Castaneda is pushed by Don Juan into a building, and when he goes out the door on the other side he is not where he should be, but in a market over a mile away. He can only assume, in his amazement, that he is hallucinating. He then finds Don Juan standing next to him, smiling. When Castaneda later decides to retrace his route, he goes to the market and finds that on the day when he though he was there the book stalls were not displayed. He must, then, have "been" there on a Sunday, even though the experience took place on a weekday.

This sort of structure, in which we have conflicting and contradictory evidence which can only be accounted for by postulating an incursion of another level of reality, is a standard one in occult fiction, as one of Mircea Eliade's occult novels (his term for them) will demonstrate. (Note, though, that Eliade at least keeps his anthropology and his fiction separate.) In *Nights at Serampore* the narrator and two friends leave a country villa for town in a car, find themselves inexplicably lost, hear screams, see people, yet when they all "come to" in the morning they are near the villa, and when they return the servants and chauffeur insist that none of them even left the house. They discover they have "been present" at a murder which took place many years before. The only explanation of the event is related to a rather mysterious religious figure who unexpectedly appears near the place, and the narrator decides that they have strayed across his sacred space. What we have, then, is a rupture of the time-space suppositions on which fiction traditionally operates.

George MacDonald's *Lilith* presents a very relevant image of this rupture. The narrator encounters a book in the library of his family house which appears to be stuck in the wall, as part of a false wall disguised as a bookcase. He can only read fragments:

> Beginnings of lines were visible on the left-hand page, and ends of lines on the other; but I could not, of course, get at the beginning and end of a single line, and was unable in what I could read, to make any guess at the sense. The mere words, however, woke in me feelings which to describe was, from their strangeness, impossible. Some dreams, some poems, some musical phrases, some pictures, woke feelings such as one never had before, new in colour and form—spiritual sensations, as it were, hitherto unproved: here some of the phrases, some of the senseless half-lines, some even of the individual words affected me in a similar fashion—as with the aroma of an idea, rousing in me a great longing to know what the poem or poems might, even yet in their mutilation, hold or suggest.[8]

Coleridge comes to mind once again. Just as in "Kubla Khan" the enchantment is not in spite of but *because* of the fragmentary quality of the phrases, the interface between different realities, and this would surely be the place to begin any exploration of the relation between the romantic and the occult. The narrator of *Lilith* later discovers that the other half of the book sticks through into another world, (this idea of a transition or interface appears elsewhere in the novel in the more traditional image of the mirror, through which one enters another world). In other words, the sentence keeps disappearing into the "other side," leaving gaps in our syntax, discontinuities, breaks of meaning, and it is significant that syntax and the sentence should here

[8]*Phantases and Lilith* (London: Victor Gollancz, Ltd., 1962), p. 198.

be used as images of the controlled and "normal" world of cause and effect.

To create the fantastic or occult one must first have the normal and the logical syntax to disrupt, and to this extent the fantastic and the occult in literature are very often dependent precisely on this power of language to disrupt or subvert itself. As Todorov says:

> If the fantastic constantly makes use of rhetorical figures, it is because it originates in them. The supernatural is born of language, it is both its consequence and its proof: not only do the devil and vampires exist only in words, but language alone enables us to conceive what is always absent: the supernatural.[9]

Doubt, or what Todorov calls "hesitation," over the status of phenomena, generated by the rupture, the broken syntax of the narration, can be generated on a large scale in terms of plot, but also on a smaller scale in individual sentences, and it is important if we are to decide what is happening in Castaneda's work to look in detail at where and how "hesitation" is generated.

He describes in *Tales of Power,* for instance, an experience while lying out in the desert at night, which he says was *neither* a vision *nor* a dream. It was a clear physical sensation but *not* related to, or caused by, anything in the environment. All these negatives cut off ways of categorizing what happened, either as a subjective experience or as an objective event. It is situated uniquely between the two. Later in the same book Don Juan puts this a different way. All experience is subjective, he suggests, but some—what we call the real and the actual—is given support by consensus, by being validated and confirmed by others. The *ambiguity* of Castaneda's experiences is generated by the fact

---

[9]T. Todorov, *The Fantastic* (Cleveland: Case Western Reserve University Press, 1973), p. 82. One could speculate, too, on the suitability of different languages to express different relations between planes of reality. It is interesting that B. L. Whorf, whose arguments for linguistic relativity, supported by material from the Hopi language, are now largely discounted by professional linguists but read and admired by many nonlinguists, was himself very interested in occult phenomena. One could see, in fact, his idealized descriptions of Hopi language as a recipe for the language which could incorporate the occult intrusions, a language which would not exclude any dimensions of reality in the first place.

that while his background and training prompt him to categorize his experiences as subjective, Don Juan, in his oblique and playful way, is confirming the experiences and giving them a consensus which gives them a claim to be *more* than subjective. Throughout Castaneda the concern to distinguish between different states of mind and different planes of reality is one which deeply affects the method of presentation. Material is presented in such a way as to re-create the ambiguities of the supposed experience, and its language and situation are being used as a novelist would use them. If we compare them with Black Elk's account of a vision in another widely read book of the same period (though recorded much earlier), we can see the difference. The five-year-old Black Elk was alone and on horseback:

> A thunderstorm was coming from where the sun goes down, and just as I was riding into the woods along a creek, there was a kingbird sitting on a limb. This was not a dream, it happened. And I was going to shoot at the kingbird with the bow my Grandfather made, when the bird spoke and said, "The clouds all over are one-sided." Perhaps it meant that all the clouds were looking at me. And then it said: "Listen! A voice is calling you!" Then I looked up at the clouds, and two men were coming there, headfirst like arrows slanting down; and as they came they sang a sacred song and the thunder was like drumming. ... I sat there gazing at them and they were coming from the place where the giant lives (north). But when they were very close to me, they wheeled about toward where the sun goes down, and suddenly they were geese. Then they were gone, and the rain came with a big wind and a roaring.[10]

Here the lack of contextualizing or explanation is initially disconcerting if we are expecting a viewpoint like our own. In fact, Black Elk adds, as a concession to *our* expectations, "This was not a dream, it happened." We are not presented with ambiguity here, as in a literary work; but those literary experiments in nonrealistic forms which present contradictory versions without the means of deciding between them, whether in the nineteenth-century romance or more recent postmodern fictions, do help us to see the ways in which sentences can fail to make sense, if by that we mean only *one* sense. Ronald Sukenick, himself a dis-

[10]*Black Elk Speaks* (New York: Pocket Books, 1972), pp. 15-16.

tinguished writer of such fictions, has suggested that Castaneda is presenting us with the *equivalent* of modern fiction (though he doesn't consider it actually fiction), in that Don Juan makes Castaneda realize that all accounts of experience are *versions* of reality, fictions, and that the common-sense or objective has no primacy, as it does in realism. The importance of the book for Sukenick is that

> he breaks down, for the alert reader, that false separation of art from life, of imagination from reality, that in our culture tends to vitiate both. This connection, which is the essence of primitive cultures, is maintained in our empiricist civilization only in the arts...and in witchcraft, the mystical cults, the various incursions of Oriental disciplines. (Noel, p. 114)

This would then imply that Castaneda is not occult (i.e., depending on a *rupture* of the accepted reality, but on its own terms) but further developed than that—a series of fictions on different levels. This raises the problem of Castaneda's insistence on documentary truth (to say nothing of his UCLA Ph.D. in anthropology for his first book).

Perhaps the real debate should be not whether Castaneda is telling the truth (Is it anthropology or fiction?), but which sort of fiction Castaneda is writing: occult (depending on realism as a framework which is temporarily ruptured) or modern nonrealist fiction, which presents multiple realities and refuses primacy to any one level—Pynchon or Burroughs, for instance. My own feeling is that Castaneda is ultimately limited to the first category, and that his movement toward occult formulae *limits* the literary possibilities of his work, as well as any spiritual dimension. This is because by focusing attention on phenomena which break the normal frame of reality, but still have to be accounted for within it, he is in fact not asserting a *separate* reality but a reality which impinges on this one and threatens it by *phenomenal* means. The attention is directed, then, to *events* which are either tricks or miracles, if seen in terms of "ordinary" reality, rather than to ideas or spiritual experiences, and Castaneda begins to run the risk that spiritualism, for instance, encountered—that phenomena which, however astounding, are fundamentally trivial do not suggest or exemplify other than a trivial spiritual or intellectual framework. This may lead us toward some under-

standing of why occult literature *is* so often trivial and kitsch —
that while it suggests a departure from realism, it is totally
parasitic upon it and has nothing to offer except for the cheap
thrill (cheap because nothing is really risked) of a temporary
departure from it.

Chronology of Important Dates

1764   Horace Walpole, *The Castle of Otranto*

1796   Matthew Gregory Lewis, *The Monk*

1818   Mary Wollstonecraft Shelley, *Frankenstein; or, The Modern Prometheus*

1819   John William Polidori, *The Vampyre*

1840   Edgar Allan Poe, *Tales of the Grotesque and Arabesque*

1847   Thomas Peckett Prest or James Malcolm Rymer, *Varney, the Vampyre*

1857   George W. Reynolds, *Wagner the Wehrwolf*

1862   Edward Bulwer-Lytton, *A Strange Story*

1866   Charles Dickens, "The Signalman"

1886   Joseph Le Fanu, *In a Glass Darkly*
           Robert Louis Stevenson, *The Strange Case of Dr. Jekyll and Mr. Hyde*

1887   H. Rider Haggard, *She*

1888   Rudyard Kipling, "The Phantom Rickshaw"

1891   Oscar Wilde, *The Picture of Dorian Gray*

1892   George du Maurier, *Peter Ibbetson*

1893   Ambrose Bierce, *Can Such Things Be?*

1894   Arthur Machen, *The Great God Pan and the Inmost Light*

1895   George MacDonald, *Lilith*

1897   Bram Stoker, *Dracula*

1898   Henry James, *The Turn of the Screw*

1904   M. R. James, *Ghost Stories of an Antiquary*

1907   Algernon Blackwood, *The Listener*

1917   Aleister Crowley, *Moonchild*

1923   Magazine *Weird Tales* begins publication (ceased 1954).

1935   Dennis Wheatley, *The Devil Rides Out*

1939   H. P. Lovecraft, *The Outsider and Others*

1959   Shirley Jackson, *The Haunting of Hill House*

1965   John Fowles, *The Magus*

1967   Ira Levin, *Rosemary's Baby*

1970   Colin Wilson, *God of the Labyrinth*

1971   William Peter Blatty, *The Exorcist*
            Thomas Tryon, *The Other*

1974   Carlos Castaneda, *Tales of Power*

1976   Anne Rice, *Interview with the Vampire*

Notes on the Editor and Contributors

MARK M. HENNELLY, JR., is Associate Professor of English at California State University, Sacramento. He is a member of the Editorial Board of the journal *Gothic* and has published extensively on nineteenth- and twentieth-century literature.

HOWARD KERR is Associate Professor of English at the University of Illinois, Chicago Circle.

H. P. LOVECRAFT (1890-1937) was one of the most important practitioners of the supernatural tale in America since Edgar Allan Poe. Many of his stories were published in the magazine *Weird Tales*. His influence was widespread, both on his contemporaries and those who have since written in the field of supernatural fiction.

PETER MESSENT, editor of this volume, has also published on Vonnegut, and lectures in the Department of American Studies at Nottingham University, England.

DAVID MURRAY is Lecturer in American Studies at Nottingham University, England. He is currently writing on the North American Indian.

JOHN R. REED is Professor of English at Wayne State University, Detroit. He is author of *Old School Ties: The Public Schools in British Literature* and *Perception and Design in Tennyson's "Idylls of the King."*

DOROTHY SCARBOROUGH (d. 1935) was Professor of English at Baylor University, Waco, Texas. Author of *Fugitive Verses, From a Southern Porch,* and *In the Land of Cotton,* she also wrote short stories, articles, and verse.

BARTON LEVI ST. ARMAND is Assistant Professor of English at Brown University, Providence, Rhode Island. Editor of the *Emerson Society Quarterly* and *Novel,* he has published on Poe, Hawthorne, and Sarah Orne Jewett.

JACK SULLIVAN is currently teaching Nineteenth Century Humanities and Twentieth Century Humanities (literature and music) at New York University in New York City.

G. R. THOMPSON is Associate Professor of English at Washington State University. He is coeditor of *Ritual, Realism, and Revolt: Major Traditions in the Drama* and author of *Poe's Fiction: Romantic Irony in the Gothic Tales.*

TZVETAN TODOROV is Attaché de Recherches at the Centre Nationale de Recherches Scientifiques in Paris. He is author of *The Poetics of Prose* and coauthor of the *Encyclopeaedic Dictionary of the Sciences of Language.*

DEVENDRA P. VARMA is Professor of English at Dalhousie University, Halifax, Nova Scotia. He has written extensively on Gothicism and the Gothic movement in eighteenth century English literature.

S. L. VARNADO is Associate Professor of American and British literature at the University of South Alabama, Mobile.

Selected Bibliography

BOOKS

Banta, Martha. *Henry James and the Occult: The Great Extension.* Bloomington, London: Indiana University Press, 1972.

Birkhead, Edith. *The Tale of Terror: A Study of the Gothic Romance.* London: Constable, 1921.

Daniels, Les. *Living in Fear: A History of Horror in the Mass Media.* New York: Scribner's, 1975.

Douglas, Drake. *Horrors!* London: John Baker, 1967.

Freud, Sigmund. "The 'Uncanny.'" In *The Standard Edition of the Complete Psychological Works,* Volume XVII. London: Hogarth Press and Institute of Psycho-Analysis, 1955.

Goss, Michael. A Sense of Wonder, a Sense of Fear: Aspects of the Supernatural in Victorian Life and Popular Literature, 1840-1900. M. Phil. dissertation, University of Nottingham, 1973.

Keppler, C. F. *The Literature of the Second Self.* Tucson: University of Arizona Press, 1972.

Penzoldt, Peter. *The Supernatural in Fiction.* London and New York: Peter Nevill, 1952.

Prickett, Stephen. *Victorian Fantasy.* Hassocks, Sussex: Harvester Press, 1979.

Saurat, Denis. *Literature and Occult Tradition: Studies in Philosophical Poetry.* Translated from the French by Dorothy Bolton. London: G. Bell and Sons, 1930.

Senior, John. *The Way Down and Out: The Occult in Symbolist Literature.* Ithaca, N.Y.: Cornell University Press, 1959.

Shreffler, Philip. *The H. P. Lovecraft Companion.* Westport, Conn.: Greenwood Press, 1977.

Sweetser, Wesley D. *Arthur Machen.* New York: Twayne Publishers, 1964.

Wolf, Leonard. *A Dream of Dracula: In Search of the Living Dead.* New York: Popular Library, 1972.

COLLECTIONS OF ESSAYS

New York Literary Forum, Vol. 4 (1980).

The Occult in Language and Literature. ed. Hermine Riffaterre. New York: 1980.